LAVONNE'S KITCHEN

Lavonne's Kitchen

LEARNING TO COOK WITH LOVE

iUniverse books may be ordered through booksellers or by contacting:

iUniverse
1663 Liberty Drive
Bloomington, IN 47403
www.iuniverse.com
844-349-9409

ISBN: 978-1-6632-4463-5 (sc)
ISBN: 978-1-6632-4465-9 (hc)
ISBN: 978-1-6632-4464-2 (e)

Library of Congress Control Number: 2022916088

Print information available on the last page.

iUniverse rev. date: 09/07/2022

LAVONNE'S KITCHEN

Learning to Cook with Love

Lavonne Fulton

DEDICATION

To my husband, Jerome Fulton. Over the past thirty-seven years of marriage, he has eaten all of my cooking, good or bad. (Although he's enjoyed most of the meals.) He has been supportive in all of my culinary endeavors, from running a catering company for over ten years to teaching people how to cook on YouTube.

He has been very complimentary and objective when I needed him to be, but never judgmental. I always get the truth about my cooking, and he gives it with love in his heart. Not only has he been supportive of my cooking career, but he has been very helpful with writing this book.

He has been a constant source of encouragement and support throughout the challenges of my career. I want to take this time to sincerely express my appreciation to him for his love and support.

TABLE OF CONTENTS

INTRODUCTION

During these times, more people are learning to cook for various reasons, such as COVID-19 or the high cost of eating out. I wanted to do my part by showing how easy it is to make restaurant-tasting food and the homecooked food that you may have grown up with in your own kitchen.

There is nothing I like more than serving a delicious, appealing meal to people. *Lavonne's Kitchen* is a cookbook that people with different skill levels can use to cook. From the beginner to the highly skilled chef, this book contains simple recipes using easy-to-find ingredients to make my versions of the most flavorful, popular, and appetizing dishes.

After years of sharing recipes in various ways and cooking for many, many people, I decided to make a cookbook to share some of those recipes around the world. This book contains a large variety of foods with over one hundred recipes, including appetizers, savory seafood, healthy foods, desserts, and much more. Crab-stuffed lobster tails and my signature dish, pasta à Lavonne, are just two of the recipes you will find in this book.

MEAT

Pulled Pork

Prep time: 15 minutes
Cooking time: 10 hours and 15 minutes
Serves 10–12

Keep pulled pork as a staple in your kitchen. Use it in sandwiches, beans, tacos, and much more.

Ingredients

6 pounds pork butt

1 large onion, divided

2 tablespoons minced garlic, divided

1 teaspoon salt

1 teaspoon pepper

1 teaspoon creole seasoning

1 teaspoon cayenne pepper

Directions

Trim most of the fat off the top of the meat. Then using a very sharp knife, make approximately eight 1-inch slits in the meat.

Thinly slice the onion.

In a small bowl, combine 1 tablespoon minced garlic and ¼ of the sliced onion . Place mixture in the slits you made in the meat. Spread the remaining garlic on top of the meat.

Place half the remaining onions in the bottom of the slow cooker. Add the meat, fat side up, and season the top with salt, pepper, creole seasoning, and cayanne pepper. Place the remaining onions on top.

Cook on low for 10 hours.

Remove the meat from the slow cooker, leaving the juice and onions in the pot. Shred the meat apart using two forks, and then put the meat back in the slow cooker pot. Stir well.

Enjoy!

Pepper Steak with Tomatoes

Prep time: 5 Minutes
Cooking time: 10 Minutes
Serves 4

Ingredients

1 pound thinly sliced top round or sirloin

1 tablespoon black pepper

1 large onion

1 large green pepper

1 large tomato (optional)

2 tablespoons vegetable oil

2 tablespoons all-purpose flour

1 (32-ounce) can beef broth

Directions

Season the steak with black pepper.

Slice the onion and green pepper into large pieces. If using the tomato, also slice it into large pieces

In a large skillet, heat the oil on high heat for one minute.

To the hot skillet, add sliced green pepper and onion. Sautee until translucent. Then add the meat and stir for 4 minutes.

To the skillet, add the flour. Stir for 30 seconds. Then add the beef broth, mixing thoroughly. If including it, add the sliced tomato.

Cover and simmer for 5 minutes.

Serve over rice and enjoy.

Meatballs in Marinara Sauce

Prep time: 15 minutes
Cooking time: 30 minutes
Serves 4–6

These meatballs are amazing. Try them with pasta or on a sub sandwich.

Ingredients
cooking spray
2 pounds ground beef
1 Egg
1 (1-ounce) package onion soup mix
⅓ cup milk
⅓ cup Italian seasoned bread crumbs
2 tablespoons minced garlic
2 tablespoons parmesan cheese
1 teaspoon Italian seasoning
1 teaspoon black pepper
marinara sauce[1]

Directions
Preheat oven to 375 degrees, and spray an 18"
x 26" sheet pan with cooking spray.

In a large bowl, combine remaining
ingredients except for marinara sauce. Mix
well.

Roll the mixture into 2-ounce balls. Place
balls on sheet pan, one inch apart. Bake for
15 minutes.

In a large bowl, combine meatballs and
marinara sauce. Place meatballs back on sheet
pan, and cook for an additional 15 minutes.
Enjoy!

---
[1]   See page 124 for recipe.

Beef Roast

Prep time: 2 minutes
Cooking time: 2 1/2 hours
Serves 4

Ingredients
1 (1-ounce) package onion soup mix, divided
2 ½ pounds angus beef
brown gravy[2]

Directions:
Preheat oven to 350 degrees.
Place half the packet of soup mix in the bottom of a baking pan. Add the meat. Spread the remaining soup mix on top of the meat. Cover with foil. Cook for 2 ½ hours.
Move meat to serving dish, leaving the juice in the bottom of the pan.
Add brown gravy to the baking pan with juice. Mix well.
Cover the meat brown gravy and juice mixture.
Enjoy!

---

[2]   See page 117 for recipe.

Short Ribs

Prep time: 10 minutes
Cooking time: 54 minutes
Serves 4–6

Ingredients

1 onion10

2 tablespoons minced garlic

2 tablespoons garlic powder

2 tablespoons black pepper

2 tablespoons seasoning salt

2 tablespoons Canadian steak seasoning

1 cup all-purpose flour, divided

2 pounds beef short ribs

3 tablespoons vegetable oil

32 ounces beef broth

2 tablespoons steak sauce

1 tablespoon brown gravy mix.

Directions:

Preheat oven to 325 degrees.

Thinly slice the onion.

In a small bowl, combine minced garlic, garlic powder, black peper, and seasoning salt. Divide spice mixture in half, placing in a second small bowl. To that second bowl, add Canadian steak seasoning, and stir until evenly incorporated.

Using ½ cup flour, evenly coat both sides of the meat. Shake off any excess.

Add oil to a large skillet, and heat on high. Once oil is heated, place meat in skillet. Cook for 2 minutes on each side.

Remove meat from skillet, and put in large baking dish. Set aside.

Add sliced onions to the remaining oil in the skillet. Sauté for 2 minutes. Add ½ cup of flour. Mix well. Cook for 1 minute, stirring constantly. Whisk in beef broth and then gravy mix. Add steak sauce and remaining spice mixture. Stir well.

Pour skillet mixture over meat. Cover, and place in oven. Bake for 45 minutes.

Enjoy!

Pineapple Sriracha Chicken

Prep time: 10 minutes
Cooking time: 47 minutes
Serves 4–6

If you like sweet and spicy, this is the perfect recipe for you. Add as little or as much sriracha sauce as you can handle.

Ingredients

1 fresh pineapple

1 medium onion

2 tablespoons fresh cilantro

2–3 tablespoons of sriracha sauce

1 teaspoon salt

1 teaspoon pepper

1 teaspoon garlic powder

6 chicken thighs (skin on)

2 tablespoons olive oil

2 tablespoons vegetable oil

Directions

Preheat oven to 350 degrees.

Dice the pineapple and onion. Chop the cilantro.

In a large bowl, combine pinapple, onion, cilantro, and sriracha. Mix well. Place mixture in a plastic bag, and set it to the side.

In a small bowl, combine salt, pepper, and garlic powder

Pull the skin back from the chicken thighs, and rub with olive oil, making sure to coat the entire thigh.

Cover in spice mixture. Save some of the spice mixture to coat the skin. Pull skin back over the thigh, and season with remaining mixture.

Add vegetable oil to a large skillet, and cook on high heat for 1 minute. Add chicken, and cook for 2–3 minutes on each side.

Place skillet with chicken in the oven. Bake for 30 minutes.

Remove excess juice from skillet. Cover chicken with pineapple mixture. Cook for an additional 5 minutes.

Change oven temperature to broil, and cook for 5 minutes.

Enjoy!

Cheesy Chicken Enchiladas

Prep time: 20 minutes
Cooking time: 20 minutes
Serves 6–8

Ingredients

2 rotisserie chicken breasts
16 ounces shredded Mexican four-cheese blend, divided
1 (28-ounce) can enchilada sauce, divided
6–8 medium-sized flour tortillas

Directions

Preheat oven to 400 degrees.

Remove the skin and bones from the chicken. Place chicken meat in a medium bowl, and shred.

To the bowl, add half the enchilada sauce and half the cheese. Combine well.

Pour half the remaining sauce into a 11" X 7" baking dish.

Lay one tortilla flat. Place the chicken mixture in the middle. Roll the tortilla, and place it in the baking dish.

Repeat until you have used all of the chicken mixture.

Spoon the remaining sauce on top of the tortillas. Sprinkle with the remaining cheese.

Place in oven, uncovered, and bake for 20 minutes.

Enjoy!

Cheesy Chicken Tortilla Casserole

Prep time: 20 minutes
Cooking time: 39 minutes
Serves 10–12

Ingredients

1 large chicken breast
1 ½ teaspoons salt, divided
4 ½ teaspoons black pepper
4 tablespoons vegetable oil, divided
1 tablespoon butter
1 medium onion, diced
3 tablespoons minced garlic
3 cups chicken stock
1 tablespoon chili powder
1 tablespoon garlic powder

1 teaspoon creole seasoning
1 teaspoon cayenne pepper
1 10 ounce can diced tomatoes with green chilies
1 10.5 ounce can cream of mushroom soup
1 10.5 ounce can cream of chicken soup
8 ounces cream cheese
2 slices provolone cheese
6 flour tortillas
2 cups shredded Mexican four-cheese blend

Directions

Preheat oven to 350 degrees.

Season the chicken with ½ teaspoon of salt and ½ teaspoon of black pepper.

Heat a large skillet on hight heat. Add 2 tablespoons of vegetable oil. Coat evenly. Add chicken, and cook for 2 minutes on both sides. Set aside.

In a second large skillet, heat butter and the remaining oil. Add onions and minced garlic. Sauté until soft. Add chicken stock, 1 teasponn salt, chili powder, garlic powder, creole seasoning, and cayenne pepper. Stir well. Add tomatoes with chilies, mushroom soup, and chicken soup. Stir well. Add cream cheese and provolone cheese, stirring until melted.

Shred the chicken breast. Add to mixture in second skillet.

Spray an 11" X 7" baking dish with cooking spray. Line the bottom with tortillas, until completely covered. Spread a layer of the cheesy chicken mixture on top. Sprinkle with shredded cheese. Add another layer of tortillas. Add more chicken mixture and shredded cheese, repeating the process until all the mixture is gone and making your final layer the shredded cheese.

Cover with foil, and bake for 25 minutes. Remove the foil and cook for an additional 10 minutes. Let cool before slicing.

If you desire, top with jalapenos, green onions, and sour cream.

Enjoy!

Rotisserie Chicken Salad

Prep time: 15 minutes
Serves 4–6

Ingredients
1 rotisserie chicken breast
2 celery stalks
¾ cup mayonnaise
1 teaspoon black pepper

Directions
Debone chicken, and shred it.
Finely dice celery.
In a large bowl, combine chicken, mayonnaise, celery, and black pepper. Stir until all ingredients are evenly combined.
Enjoy!

Grilled Chicken Kabobs

Prep time: 2 hours
Cooking time: 1 hour and 15 minutes
Serves 4–6

Ingredients

skewers

water

1 large red onion

1 green bell pepper

1 yellow bell pepper

1 red bell pepper

3 ears corn

8 ounces button mushrooms

1 pound boneless, skinless chicken breast or thighs

8 ounces cherry tomatoes

1 (8-ounce) bottle Italian dressing

1 teaspoon black pepper

Directions

Lay skewers flat in a 11"X 7" baking dish . Cover with water, and soak for 30 minutes.

While the skewers are soaking, Boil the corn for 30 minutes also.

Evenly slice onion and bell peppers into large pieces.

Clean the mushrooms with a wet paper towel.

Dice the chicken into 1-inch cubes.

Then cut the corn it into 2-inch pieces.

Add the chicken, onion, bell peppers, corn, mushrooms, and tomatoes to the skewers, alternating ingredients. Make the kabobs as long or short as you like.

In a large, rectangular, plastic container, add Italian dressing. Soak the skewers in the dressing for 1 hour, rotating every 15 minutes.

Remove the skewers from the dressing and sprinkle with black pepper.

Place skewers on a 400 degree preheated grill. Cook for 45 minutes, rotating every 10 minutes. Remove from Grill. Enjoy!

Chicken Potpie

Prep time: 15 minutes
Cooking time: 1 hour
Serves 2–4

Ingredients

1 large onion
2 celery stalks
2 Idaho potatoes
1 ½ pounds boneless, skinless chicken breast or thighs
2 teaspoons salt
1 teaspoon black pepper
1 teaspoon garlic powder
1 teaspoon onion powder
½ teaspoon Italian seasoning
1 tablespoon olive oil

2 carrots
½ cup frozen green peas
⅓ cup unsalted butter
⅓ cup all-purpose flour
3 cups chicken stock
2 tablespoons thyme
1/2 cup heavy cream
1 14.1 ounce rollable pie crust
1 17.3 ounce package puff pastry

Directions

Preheat the oven to 400 degrees.

Finely dice the carrots,onion and celery. Peel and dice the potatoes.

Cut chicken into 1-inch squares. Season with salt, black pepper, garlic powder, onion powder, and Italian seasoning.

In a large pot, heat olive oil over medium-high heat for 1 minute. Add chicken, and cook for 5 minutes, stirring occasionally.

To the pot, add onion, celery, potatoes, carrots, peas, and butter. Stir until butter melts. Whisk in flour. Cook for 1 minute. Add chicken stock and thyme. Bring to a boil. Reduce heat, and cook for 15 minutes.

Stir heavy cream into the pot. Simmer for 10 minutes.

Unroll your pie crust, and put in a 12" cake pan

Unfold 1 sheet of the puff pastry.

Pour mixture from the pot into the cake pan. Top with puff pastry. Cut four slits into the pastry.

Place cake pan on a 11" X 26" baking sheet . Bake for 20 minutes or until top is golden brown.

Enjoy!

Roasted Smoked Turkey Leg

Prep time: 10 minutes
Cooking time: 2 hours
Serves 2–4

Ingredients:

½ medium onion

½ cup water

1 smoked turkey leg

2 tablespoons minced garlic

1 teaspoon creole seasoning

1 teaspoon black pepper

Directions:

Preheat the oven to 375 degrees.

Slice the onion into large pieces.

Add water to the bottom of a 11" X 7" baking dish. Add the turkey leg. Top with onion slices, minced garlic, creole seasoning, and black pepper. Cover with foil, and bake for 2 hours.

Enjoy!

Cheesy Spinach Stuffed Chicken

Prep time: 10 minutes
Cooking time: 45 minutes
Serves 4–6

Ingredients

1 medium onion

4 tablespoons vegetable oil, divided

2 pounds fresh spinach

4 teaspoons salt

4 teaspoons black pepper

2 teaspoons garlic powder

1 large boneless, skinless chicken breast

1 cup mozzarella cheese

1 cup feta cheese

Directions

Dice onion.

Using a meat mallet or a large spoon, beat the chicken until flat (approximately 1/4 inch).

Cut into 4 pieces.

In a large skillet, heat 2 tablespoons of oil on medium heat. Add onion and spinach. Sauté for 5 minutes.

While the onion and spinach cook, combine salt, black pepper, and garlic powder in a small bowl.

Add half the spice mixture to the skillet. Stir well. Drain and set aside.

Season chicken on both sides with the other half of the spice mixture.

In a medium bowl, combine the mozzarella and feta cheeses.

To another large skillet, add the remaining oil and 2 pieces of chicken. Cook for 2 minutes on each side.

Place 1 tablespoon of the spinach mixture on top of the left side of the chicken. Add cheese mixture on top of spinach. Cover skillet with a lid, and cook for 3–5 minutes.

Fold the right side of chicken onto the left side, covering the spinach and cheese. Press down on the chicken.

Remove from pan.

Repeat until all four pieces are done.

Enjoy!

Chicken Stir-Fry

Prep time: 10 minutes
Cooking time: 20 minutes
Serves 4–6

Ingredients

2 boneless, skinless chicken breasts
2 large carrots
1 large onion
1 green bell pepper
1 red bell pepper
¼ cup soy sauce, divided in half

2 teaspoons garlic powder, divided in half
2 teaspoons black pepper, divided in half
1 teaspoon red pepper flakes
2 tablespoons vegetable oil
3 cups broccoli
1 4 ounce can mushrooms

Directions

Dice chicken into 1" squares.

Julienne carrots, onions, and bell peppers.

To a plastic bag, add chicken, ½ of soy sauce, 1 teaspoon of garlic powder, 1 teaspoon of black pepper, and ½ teaspoon of red pepper flakes. Marinate for 10 minutes.

Add oil to a large skillet, and heat on high for 1 minute. Place marinated chicken in the skillet. Cook for 3 minutes, stirring constantly.

Add Carrots. Cook for 3–4 minutes while stirring.

Add onion, bell peppers, and broccoli. Add the remaining soy sauce, garlic powder, black pepper, and red pepper flakes. Combine well. Add mushrooms. Cover and cook for an addition 5 minutes.

Enjoy!

Pineapple Chicken Fried Rice

Prep time: 1 hour and 10 minutes
Cooking time: 15 minutes
Serves 4–6

Ingredients

2 chicken breasts

6 tablespoons soy sauce, divided

1 medium yellow onion

2 green onions

1 teaspoon garlic powder, divided

1 teaspoon black pepper, divided

4 tablespoons vegetable oil, divided

1 cup pineapple tidbits

1 egg

3 cups rice, leftover

Directions

To a large bowl, add chicken breasts and half the soy sauce. Marinate for 1 hour.

Finely dice the yellow onion. Slice the green onions into approx. ¼" pieces.

Season the marinated chicken with half the garlic powder and half the black pepper.

In a large skillet, heat half the oil over high heat. Add the chicken breast. Cook for 3 minutes on each side.

Remove the chicken. Dice it, and place in a large bowl. Add the pineapple tidbits, and set aside.

In a small bowl, scramble the egg. Set aside.

In a second large skillet, heat the remaining oil over high heat for 45 seconds. Add the onions, and cook for 1 minute, stirring often.

Add the egg to the skillet, stirring constantly. Add the rice. Combine well. Cook for 2 minutes.

To the skillet, add the chicken and pineapple mixture, the remaining soy sauce, and half the green onions. Season with the remaining garlic powder and the remaining black pepper. Mix well. Cook for 3 minutes.

Top with the remaining green onions.

Enjoy!

Mango Salsa, Chicken, and Rice

Prep time: 15 minutes
Cooking time: 30 minutes
Serves 6

Ingredients
2 tablesoons salt
1 tablespoon black pepper
½ teaspoon creole seasoning
2 large boneless, skinless chicken breasts
2 tablespoons vegetable oil
2 cups spicy, chunky salsa
2 cups white rice
2 cups chicken broth
1 cup mango, diced

Directions
In a small bowl, combine the salt, black pepper, and creole seasoning.
Thinly slice the chicken into six pieces. Season with half the spice mixture
Add oil to a large skillet, and cook on high heat for approximately 1 minute.
Add the chicken to the skillet.Cook for 1 ½ minutes on each side. Place chicken on a plate, and set aside.
Add rice, mango, salsa, chicken broth, and remaining spice mixture to skillet. Stir well. Place chicken back in the skillet. Reduce heat to low. Cover and simmer for half an hour.
Enjoy!

Smothered Pork Chops

Prep time: 5 minutes
Cooking time: 25 minutes
Serves 6–8

Ingredients

2 teaspoons salt

2 teaspoons creole seasoning

2 teaspoons garlic powder

1 teaspoon onion powder

1 teaspoon black pepper

8 pork chops

2 cups flour, divided

2 cups vegetable oil

1 large onion, sliced

32 ounces chicken broth

Directions

In a small bowl, combine salt, creole seasoning, garlic powder, onion powder, and black pepper.

Pat meat with a paper towel until dry. Season both sides with half the spice mixture.

Place 1 ½ cups of flour in a large ziplock bag. Add two pork chops to the bag, and shake until chops are completely covered. Shake off any excess flour. Set the floured pork chops aside. Add two more pork chops to the bag. Repeat until all pork chops are floured.

Add oil to a large skillet, and cook over high heat for approximately 1 minute.

Place 2–3 pork chops in the skillet. Do not overcrowd the skillet. Cook 2 minutes on each side or until browned. Remove the pork chops from the skillet, and set aside. Repeat until all pork chops are cooked.

Add the onion slices to the oil, and stir well. Cook until the onions are translucent.

Add the remaining flour to the skillet. Whisk for approximately 1 minute. Then whisk in the chicken broth. Add the remaining spice mixture, and whisk well.

Put pork chops back into the skillet. Reduce heat to low. Cover and cook for 25 minutes.

Enjoy!

Peach BBQ Pork Loin

Prep time: 5 minutes
Cooking time: 1 hour 5 minutes
Serves 4–6

Ingredients
1 15.25 ounce can diced peaches
1 (12-ounce) bottle barbeque sauce
3–4 pounds pork loin
2 tablespoons olive oil
2 teaspoons salt
2 teaspoons black pepper

Directions
Preheat oven to 350 degrees

In a medium saucepan, combine peaches and barbeque sauce. Cook over medium heat for 5 minutes, stirring occasionally. Set aside.

Coat pork loin with olive oil on both sides. Season all over with salt and pepper.

Put pork loin in an 11" X 7" baking dish. Cover with foil, and bake for 45 minutes.

Remove baking dish from oven. Keep covered, and let sit for 15 minutes.

Slice the pork loin. Pour the sauce on top.

Enjoy!

Pork Chops and Peppers

Prep time: 15 minutes
Cooking time: 25 minutes
Serves 4

Ingredients

1 onion
1 green bell pepper
1 red bell pepper
1 yellow bell pepper
1 orange bell pepper
2 tablespoons olive oil

1 tablespoon minced garlic, divided
1 ½ teaspoons black pepper, divided
1 ½ teaspoons salt, divided
1 teaspoon creole seasoning, divided
4 large pork chops

Directions

Dice the onions and peppers. Set aside.

Heat one tablespoon oil in a large skillet.

In a small bowl, combine 1 teaspoon each of minced garlic, black peper, salt, and creole seasoning. Season both sides of the pork chops with the spice mixture.

Add pork chops to the hot skillet. Sear each side for 2 minutes.

Heat the oven to broil. Place pork chops in a 4.8 quart baking dish, and cook for 5 minutes.

In a second skillet, heat remaining oil. Add onions and peppers. Season with the remaining minced garlic, the remaining salt, and the remaining black pepper. Sauté until soft, stirring often.

Remove the pork chops from the oven. Pour peppers and onions on top. Cover baking dish with a lid.

Heat the oven to 400 degrees. Put the pork chops back in the oven, and cook for 10 minutes.

Enjoy!

Cheese-and-Asparagus-Stuffed Chicken

Prep time: 10 minutes
Cooking time: 25 minutes
Serves 4

The presentation of this recipe makes it the prefered dish to serve at a fancy dinner party. It is very flavorful and guaranteed to impress.

Ingredients

1 pound fresh asparagus

2 tablespoons olive oil, divided

1 teaspoon minced garlic

½ teaspoon black pepper, divided

½ teaspoon salt, divided

1 large chicken breast, sliced thin

½ cup shredded mozzarella cheese

2 wooden bamboo skewers

Directions

Preheat oven to 375 degrees.

Wash the asparagus. Trim 1 inch from the bottoms, and place them on a baking sheet. Pat them dry, and brush with tablespoon olive oil. Roll them around until fully covered. Season with minced garlic, ½ of the salt, and ½ of the black pepper. Thinly slice asparagus into four even pieces.

Using a paper towel, pat the chicken dry. Place the chicken on a cutting board, and cover with plastic wrap. Using a meat mallet or a large spoon, beat the chicken until flat or approximately ¼ inch.

Remove the plastic wrap, and season both sides of the chicken with remaining salt and black pepper.

Add remaining olive oil to a large skillet, and cook on high heat for approximately 1 minute.

Add the chicken to the skillet, and cook for 2 minutes on each side.

Place chicken on a second baking sheet. Add cheese and four asparagus on top. Wrap the chicken around the asparagus, and close using skewers.

Place chicken in the oven, and bake for 15 minutes. Remove chicken from the oven.

Enjoy!

Air-Fried Pork Chops

Prep time: 5 minutes
Cooking time: 10 minutes
Serves 4

Ingredients
8 pork chops
1 teaspoon onion powder
1 teaspoon black pepper
1 teaspoon salt
1 teaspoon creole seasoning
1 teaspoon garlic powder
2 cups flour
cooking spray

Directions
Pat pork chops dry with a paper towel. Season both sides with onion powder, black pepper, salt, creole seasoning, and garlic powder.

Place flour in a large ziplock bag. Add two pork chops to the bag, and shake until completely covered. Shake off any excess flour. Remove pork chops. Set aside. Add two more pork chops to the bag, and repeat until all pork chops are floured.

Lightly spray one side of the pork chops with cooking spray. Place pork chops in the air fryer, oil side up. Cook for 10 minutes.

Flip pork chops. Spray top side with cooking oil, and cook for another 10 minutes.

Remove pork chops from the air fryer, and place them on a plate lined with paper towels.

Enjoy!

SEAFOOD

Crab-and-Shrimp-Stuffed Salmon

Prep time: 10 minutes
Cooking time: 30 minutes
Serves 4

Ingredients

2 green onions

3 teaspoons lemon pepper

3 teaspoons creole seasoning

3 teaspoons salt

½ pound raw shrimp, deveined

2 tablespoons olive oil

4 ½ tablespoons butter, divided

2 pounds fresh salmon

1 (8-ounce) package cream cheese

1 lemon

8 ounces crabmeat

1 tablespoon parmesan reggiano cheese

Directions

Preheat the oven to 400 degrees.

Slice green onions into thin pieces.

In a small bowl, lemon pepper, creole seasoning, and salt.

Season the shrimp with ⅓ of the seasoning mixture.

In a skillet, heat the oil and half the butter over medium heat. Add Shrimp. Cook for 1 minute on each side.

Remove the shrimp from the skillet, and cut into small pieces.

Slice the salmon into two 3-inch wide strips. Season on side with ⅓ the seasoning mixture.

Add cream cheese to a medium bowl. Squeeze the juice from the lemon on top. Add the green onion slices, the remaining seasoning mixture, the crabmeat, the shrimp, and the parmesan reggiano cheese. Mix well.

Spread crab mixture on top of one piece of salmon.[3] Top with another piece of salmon.

In a large skillet, melt 2 tablespoons of butter over medium heat.

Place the stuffed salmon in the hot skillet. Cover and put in the oven for 15 minutes.

Remove the skillet from oven. Uncover and add the remaining ½ tablespoon of butter on top of the salmon.

Recover and place the skillet back in the oven for an additional 15 minutes.

Remove from oven, and enjoy!

---

[3]   If any mixture is left, put it in a small dish, and bake for 15 minutes. Use it as a dip.

Salmon with Pineapples and Peppers

Prep time: 10 minutes
Cooking time: 12 minutes
Serves 4–6

Ingredients

½ cup pineapple

½ yellow onion

½ green bell pepper

½ red bell pepper

½ yellow bell pepper

½ orange bell pepper

3 pounds fresh salmon

2 tablespoons olive oil, divided in half

1 ½ teaspoons black pepper

1 ½ teaspoons salt

1 teaspoon lemon pepper

1 tablespoon minced garlic

Directions

Dice the pineapple, onions, and bell peppers. Set aside.

Cut salmon into four pieces.

In a large skillet, heat 1 tablespoon of the oil on high heat.

Season both sides of salmon with the black pepper, salt, and lemon pepper.

Add salmon to the hot skillet. Sear on each side for 3 minutes.

In a second large skillet, add the remaining oil. Heat over medium heat. Add the onions, bell peppers, pineapples, and minced garlic. Sauté until soft, stirring often.

Pour pepper mixture on top of salmon.

Enjoy!

Jumbo Lump Crab Cakes

Prep time: 5 minutes
Cooking time: 6 minutes
Feeds 4–5

Ingredients

1 (1-pound) can of jumbo lump crabmeat
2 green onions, sliced
1 large egg
1 cup bread crumbs
¼ cup vegetable oil

1 teaspoon old bay seasoning
1 teaspoon black pepper
1 teaspoon garlic powder
1 teaspoon lemon pepper

Directions

To a large bowl, add all ingredients. Mix well.

Form five patties.

Heat a cast-iron skillet over medium heat. Add oil and patties. Cook for 3 minutes each side.

Place patties on a paper towel, and allow excess oil to drain.

Enjoy!

Cajun-Fried Shrimp

Prep time: 45 minutes
Cooking time: 10 minutes
Serves 4

Ingredients

2 tablespoons yellow mustard

2 tablespoons hot sauce

1 pound shrimp, peeled and deveined

2 eggs

2 cups all-purpose flour

1 tablespoon creole seasoning

½ tablespoon salt

½ teaspoon garlic powder

½ gallon vegetable oil

Directions

In a large bowl, add the mustard, hot sauce, and shrimp. Stir until well coated. Refrigerate for half an hour.

In a small bowl, scramble the eggs. Pour over the shrimp, and mix well.

In a large plastic bag, combine the flour, creole seasoning, salt, and garlic powder. Add shrimp, and shake until fully coated. Remove the shrimp, shaking off any excess flour mixture.

In a large skillet, heat the oil to 350 degrees.

Add half the shrimp to the oil. Cook until golden brown. Remove shrimp, and place on a plate lined with paper towels. Repeat with the remaining shrimp.

Enjoy!

Tuscan Salmon

Prep time:10 minutes
Cooking time: 10 minutes
Serves 4–6

Ingredients

2 pounds fresh salmon

1 tablespoon lemon pepper, divided

1 tablespoon salt

1 tablespoon black pepper

1 lemon

1 tablespoon vegetable oil

2 tablespoons butter

2 tablespoons minced garlic

1 cup heavy whipping cream

3 heaping tablespoons sun-dried tomatoes

1 14.5 ounce can chicken broth or white wine

½ pound fresh spinach

¼ cup parmesan reggiano cheese

Directions

Slice the salmon into 2-inch wide slices. Season with salt, pepper, and half the lemon pepper. Squeeze the juice from the lemon on top.

Add the oil to a large skillet, and heat on high. Add Salmon. Cook for 1 ½ minutes on each side. Remove salmon, and set aside.

Melt the butter in the skillet. Add the garlic, and stir well. Reduce heat to medium.

Add the cream to the skillet. Stir well. Add the tomatoes and broth or wine. Stir well, and cook for 2 minutes.

Add the spinach to the skillet, and cook for 5 minutes, mixing often.

Add the cheese and remaining lemon pepper to the skillet, and stir. Return the salmon to the skillet. Cover fish with sauce. Cook for 3–4 minutes.

Enjoy!

Lobster Flatbread Pizza

Prep time: 15 minutes
Cooking time: 10 minutes
Serves 4

Ingredients

2 raw lobster tails

¼ cup butter

lavash bread, approximately 8 1/2" x 11"

½ teaspoon lemon pepper

1 tablespoon garlic paste

¼ cup Mexican cheese blend

1 cup multicolored cherry tomatoes

¼ cup mozzarella cheese

Directions

Preheat the oven to 425 degrees.

Remove the lobster tails from shell, and cut into small chunks.

Melt the butter in the microwave. Spread half on the bread.

In a medium bowl, combine the lobster chunks, lemon pepper, and the remaining half of the butter. Mix well, and set aside.

Spread the garlic paste on the buttered bread. Cover with Mexican cheese blend.

Cut the cherry tomatoes in half. Place on bread, flat side down.

Add the lobster to the bread, and cover with mozzarella cheese. Bake for 10 minutes.

Slice and enjoy!

Cheesy Spinach-Stuffed Salmon

Prep time: 10 minutes
Cooking time: 15 minutes
Serves 6

Ingredients

baking oil spray
3 ounces olive oil, divided
1 large onion, diced
2 pounds fresh spinach
8 ounces cream cheese
½ cup parmesan cheese

2 teaspoon salt, divided
2 teaspoon black pepper, divided
1 teaspoon garlic powder
6 pounds salmon (skin on)
2 ounces lemon juice

Directions

Preheat oven to 400 degrees, and spray a baking pan with baking oil spray.

In a large skillet, heat 1 tablespoon olive oil Add onion, and cook until translucent, stirring consistently.

Add spinach to the onions, and cook until completely wilted, stirring consistently.

To the onions and spinach, add the cream cheese, parmesan cheese, one teaspoon salt, one teaspoon black pepper, and garlic powder. Stir thoroughly, and set aside.

Slice salmon into 2-inch wide pieces. Then slice along the side to create a pocket. Season with remaining salt, black pepper, and lemon juice.

To a second large skillet, add two tablespoons oil, and heat over medium heat. Add salmon, skin side down. Cook for 1 minute.

Remove salmon from the skillet, and stuff with 2 tablespoons of the spinach mixture. Place stuffed salmon in a 17.25 X 10.75" oiled baking pan. Repeat until all pieces of salmon are stuffed.

Place salmon in the oven, and bake for 15 minutes.

Remove from oven, and enjoy!

Shrimp Scampi

Prep time: 5 minutes
Cooking time: 3 minutes
Serves 4

Ingredients

1 stick butter

1 tablespoon minced garlic

1 pound shrimp, peeled, deveined, and cooked

1 tablespoon salt

1 teaspoon black pepper

8 ounces white wine

2 tablespoons chopped fresh parsley

Directions

In a large skillet, melt butter over medium heat.

Add the garlic to the skillet. Cook for 30 seconds, stirring constantly.

Add the shrimp, salt, and black pepper to the garlic. Cook for 1 minute, stirring constantly.

Add the white wine and parsley to the shrimp, and stir.

Enjoy alone, or serve over pasta.

Seafood Potpie

Prep time: 15 minutes
Cooking time: 1 hour
Serves 2–4

Ingredients

2 celery stalks
1 large onion
2 Idaho potatoes
8 ounces small shrimp, cooked
2 teaspoons salt
1 teaspoon black pepper
1 teaspoon garlic powder
1 teaspoon onion powder
½ teaspoon Italian seasoning
1 tablespoon olive oil

½ cup frozen green peas and carrots
⅓ cup unsalted butter
⅓ cup all-purpose flour
3 cups chicken stock
2 tablespoons thyme
½ cup heavy cream
1 14.1 ounce rollable pie crust
1 11.36 ounce box prepackaged cheddar biscuit mix, made into dough
1 16 ounce can jumbo lump crabmeat

Directions

Preheat oven to 400 degrees.
Finely dice the celery stalks and onion. Peel and dice the potatoes.
Season shrimp with salt, black pepper, garlic powder, onion powder, and Italian seasoning.
In a large skillet, heat olive oil over medium-high heat. Add shrimp, and cook for 5 minutes, stirring occasionally. Set aside.
In a large pot add celery, onions, potatoes, peas and carrots, and butter. Stir until butter melts. Whisk in flour, and cook for 1 minute.
Add the chicken stock and thyme to the pot. Bring to a boil. Reduce heat to a simmer, and cook for 15 minutes.
Stir the heavy whipping cream into the pot. Simmer for 10 minutes.
Add crabmeat and cooked shrimp.
Roll out the pie crust, and put it in a 9" round cake pan. Pour filling from the pot into the cake pan.
Make biscuit dough according to box directions. Top with biscuit dough.
Place the cake pan on a 9" X 14" baking sheet and bake for 20 minutes or until top is golden brown.
Enjoy!

Crawfish Étouffée

Prep time: 10 minutes
Cooking time: 20 minutes
Serves 4

Ingredients

2 tablespoons vegetable oil

½ cup diced green bell pepper

½ cup diced onion

½ cup diced celery

1 stick unsalted butter

1 cup flour

2 cups chicken broth

8 ounces crawfish tails

4 cups cooked rice

Directions

In a large skillet, heat the oil on high for 1 minute. Add the peppers, onions, and celery. Cook for approximately 5 minutes or until soft.

In a medium pot, melt the butter on low heat . Stir in the flour. Cook until it turns chocolate brown in color, stirring continuously.

Slowly add the chicken broth, stirring continuously.

Add the bell peppers, onions, and celery. Combine well. Add the crawfish, and stir. Simmer for 15 minutes.

Serve over rice, and enjoy!

Seafood Foil Packets

Prep time: 10 minutes
Cooking time: 45 minutes
Serves 4

Ingredients

½ stick butter

2 ears of corn

3 large red potatoes

1 ½ pounds crab legs

1 pound shrimp

2 tablespoons old bay seasoning

1 ½ teaspoons black pepper

1 ½ teaspoons salt

1 ½ teaspoons garlic powder

1 teaspoon lemon pepper

Directions

Preheat oven to 375 degrees.

Place the butter in a microwave-safe cup, and melt it in the microwave.

Cut the corn into 3-inch pieces. Cut the potatoes into 1-inch chunks. Break the crab legs apart at the joints.

In the middle of 4 14"sheets of foil, place four shrimp, one piece of corn, 1/4 cup of potatoes, and four crab legs. Repeat until all of the shrimp, corn, potatoes, and crab legs are used.

Pour 3 tablespoons of melted butter in each foil packet, and season with old bay seasoning, black pepper, salt, garlic powder, and lemon pepper.

Fold the foil closed, and place the packets on a 17" X 12" baking sheet . Bake for 45 minutes.

Remove the foil packets from the oven, and put them on a plate. Open the packets, and pour the remaining butter on top of each.

Enjoy!

Crab-Stuffed Lobster Tail

Prep time: 10 minutes
Cooking time: 6 minutes
Serves 4

Ingredients

4 lobster tails
2 green onions
1 (8-ounce) can jumbo lump crab
2 eggs
½ cup bread crumbs

2 tablespoons olive oil
1 ½ teaspoons black pepper
1 ½ teaspoons salt
1 teaspoon old bay seasoning
1 teaspoon lemon pepper

Directions

Pull lobster meat out of the shell until the meat rests on top.

Slice the green onions.

In a medium sized bowl, combine the crab, eggs, bread crumbs, olive oil, black pepper, salt, old bay seasoning, and lemon pepper.

Make a ball out of a quarter of the mixture, and place on top of one lobster tail. Repeat for the other three lobster tails.

Place the lobster tails on a baking sheet. Broil for 4–6 minutes or until golden brown.

Enjoy!

SOUPS

Chicken Broth from Scratch

Prep time: 5 minutes
Cooking time: 30 minutes
Makes 3 cups

Ingredients

2 pounds chicken with the skin on
3 cups water
2 celery stalks

1 cup carrots
1 tablespoon salt

Directions

To a large pot, add all ingredients.
Simmer on low-medium heat for half an hour.
Strain broth, and let cool.
Enjoy!

Creamy Chicken and Noodles

Prep time:10 minutes
Cooking time:65 minutes
Serves 6–8

Ingredients

2 celery stalks

½ onion

½ pound carrots

1 large boneless, skinless chicken breast

32 ounces water

1 teaspoon salt

½ teaspoon black pepper

1 (16-ounce) bag egg noodles

1 (10-ounce) can cream of mushroom soup

1 (10-ounce) can cream of chicken soup

Directions

Add celery, onion, and carrots to a food processor, and chop until they are very small.

In a large pot, add the chicken breast, water, celery, onion, carrots, salt, and black pepper. Cook on medium heat for 45 minutes.

Remove the chicken from the pot, and set aside.

Add the noodles to the pot. Cook for 10 minutes.

Cut the chicken into small pieces, and return it to the pot. Add both cans of soup, and stir well. Heat over low heat for 10 minutes.

Enjoy!

Vegetable Beef Soup

Prep Time:15 minutes
Cook Time: One hour and 50 minutes
Serves 6 -8

Ingredients

2 pound roast
1 1.8 ounce package onion soup mix
32 ounces water, divided
3 medium white potatoes
1 onion
1 green bell pepper
1 celery stalk
½ pound carrots
1 teaspoon minced garlic

¼ cup vegetable oil
1 tablespoon salt
1 tablespoon black pepper
1 10 ounce can diced tomatoes with green chilies
1 15.25 ounce can whole corn
1 14.5 ounce can green beans
2 tablespoons worcestershire sauce
2 tablespoons steak sauce

Directions

Preheat oven to 375 degrees.

In a 4.8 quart baking dish, cover roast with onion soup mix. Add ½ cup water. Cover with foil, and bake for 1 hour.

Peel and dice potatoes. Boil for 15 minutes. Drain. Set aside.

Dice onion, green bell pepper, celery, and carrots small.

In a medium skillet, sauté celery, onion, pepper, carrots, and garlic in vegetable oil for 5 minutes. Season with salt and black pepper.

Once roast is cooked, remove from oven. Shred meat.

In a large stock pot, add sauteed vegetables, potatoes, corn, green beans, tomatoes, shredded roast, worcestershire sauce, salt, black pepper, steak sauce and the remaining water.

Cook on low heat for 30 minutes.

Enjoy!

Creamy, Smokey Carrot Soup

Prep time: 15 minutes
Cooking time: 30 minutes
Serves 6–8

Ingredients

32 ounces baby carrots
6 Cups water for boiling
1 ½ cups additional water
½ cup diced onion
1 tablespoon mince garlic
½ teaspoon smoked paprika

½ teaspoon oregano
½ teaspoon basil
½ teaspoon salt
½ teaspoon black pepper
½ stick butter
½ cup heavy whipping cream

Directions

Heat a large pot over high heat. Add the carrots and enough water to cover the tops of them(6 cups). Add the diced onion and minced garlic. Season with the smoked paprika, oregano, basil, salt, and black pepper. Stir and boil until carrots are soft. To test this, poke with a fork.

Strain the carrots, saving the liquid.

Put the carrots and ¼ cup of the strained liquid in a blender. Blend until they are a puree consistency.

Put the pureed carrots back in the pot, and heat over medium heat. Add the remaining strained liquid. Stir well. While stirring continuously, add the remaining 1 ½ cups water, the butter, and the heavy whipping cream. Simmer on low heat for 5 minutes.

Enjoy!

Seafood Gumbo

Prep time: 55 minutes
Cooking time: 1 hour and 5 minutes
Serves 8–10

This is one of my signature dishes. It has more seafood than most seafood gumbo recipes, and it has a few surprise ingredients. If you like gumbo, this is sure to become your favorite gumbo recipe.

Ingredients

1 Polish sausage

1 andouille sausage

2 onions, divided

2 celery stalks

1 green bell pepper

1 tablespoon olive oil

16 ounces frozen okra

8 ½ cups water, divided

1 teaspoon black pepper, divided

1 teaspoon creole seasoning, divided

½ pound shrimp

1 stick butter

½ cup all-purpose flour

32 ounces chicken broth

1 10 ounce can diced tomatoes with green chilies

1 teaspoon cayenne pepper

1 teaspoon old bay seasoning

1 teaspoon garlic powder

1 bay leaf

½ pound crab legs

½ pound crab claws

½ pound crawfish tails

1 cup leftover roast beef (optional) *see my roast beef recipe on page 5*

1 cup cooked rice per serving of gumbo

Directions

Preheat oven to 350 degrees.

Slice the Polish and andouille sausages into ¼-inch thick rounds.

Dice one onion, and set aside.

Dice the remaining onion, the celery stalks, and the green bell pepper. Place in a 4.8 quart baking dish, and combine. Add the sausages. Stir and cover. Place in the oven for 25 minutes.

To a large pot, add the olive oil and the diced onion that was set aside. Sauté the onion for 5 minutes on low heat.

To the pot, add the okra, ½ cup water, half the black pepper, and half the creole seasoning. Cook for 30 minutes. Without draining the pot, use a potato masher to mash the okra.

Peel, devein, and remove the tail shells from the shrimp. Add the tail shells to a pot with the remaining 8 cups water. Boil for 5 minutes, and then set aside to cool.

Strain the shells from the shrimp stock. Throw away the shells. Set the stock aside.

In a medium pot melt the butter over medium-low heat. Whisk in the flour. Cook for 30 minutes or until the roux turns dark brown, whisking often.

To a large stock pot, add the chicken broth, sausage mixture, roux, okra, and canned tomatoes. Season with the cayenne pepper, old bay seasoning, garlic powder, bay leaves, the remaining ½ teaspoon black pepper, and the remaining ½ teaspoon creole seasoning. If using the optional roastbeef, add it now. Cook for 1 hour over low heat.

Break apart the crab legs at the joints. Add the crab legs and claws to the pot. Cook for 10 minutes.

Add the crawfish tails and the shrimp to the pot, and cook for 10 additional minutes.

Remove the bay leaf.

Serve over rice.

Enjoy!

Chicken and Sausage Gumbo

Prep time:1 hour
Cooking time: 1 hour and 30 minutes
Serves 8–10

Ingredients

3 Polish or andouille sausages
2 tablespoons creole seasoning
2 tablespoons minced garlic
2 teaspoons salt
1 teaspoon black pepper
1 teaspoon crushed red pepper
2 large onions, divided
3 celery stalks
1 green bell pepper
2 cups boneless, skinless chicken breasts or thighs

½ cup and 1 tablespoon olive oil, divided
16 ounces frozen okra
½ cup water
½ cup of flour
1 stick butter
32 ounces chicken broth
1 10 ounce can diced tomatoes with green chilies
1 bay leaf
10 cups cooked rice

Directions

Prep:

Preheat oven to 350 degrees.

Slice the sausages into ¼-inch thick rounds.

Dice one onion, the celery stalks, and the green pepper. Place in a 4.8 quart baking dish . Add the sausage, and combine. Cover the baking dish, and place in the oven. Cook for 25 minutes.

While the sausages are cooking, dice the other onion, and set aside.

In a small bowl, combine the creole seasoning, minced garlic, salt, black pepper, and crushed red pepper. Mix well. Cut the chicken into small cubes. Season with ⅓ the spice mixture.

Heat ¼ cup oil in a skillet. Add the chicken. Cook for 4 minutes, and set aside.

In a medium pot, place 1 tablespoon olive oil, and heat over medium heat for 1 minute. Add the diced onion that was set aside. Sauté it for 5 minutes.

To the pot, add the okra, water, and ⅓ the spice mixture. Cook for 30 minutes.

Without draining, use a potato masher to mash the okra. Set aside.

In a saucepan, combine the flour and butter. Cook over medium-low heat for 30 minutes or until roux turns dark brown, whisking often.

Cook:

To a large stock pot, add the cooked chicken, chicken broth, sausage mixture, okra, canned tomatoes, and roux. Season with the remaining spice mixture and the bay leaf. Cook for 1 hour and 30 minutes over low heat.

Remove the bay leaf.

Serve over rice, and enjoy!

French Onion Soup

Prep time: 15 minutes
Cooking time: 10 minutes
Serves 6–8

Ingredients

1 French baguette
1 cup gruyere cheese
1 cup shredded mozzarella cheese
3 large onions
1 stick butter
2 tablespoons olive oil

1 teaspoon black pepper
1 teaspoon salt
1 teaspoon Italian seasoning
¼ teaspoon garlic powder
64 ounces beef broth

Directions

Cut the bread into ¼-inch thick pieces.

Shred the gruyere cheese, and combine it with the mozzarella cheese in a medium bowl.

Slice onions.

Place butter in a large saucepan. Melt it over medium heat (approx. 2 minutes).

Add olive oil and onions to the saucepan. Season with the black pepper, salt, Italian seasoning, and garlic powder.

Stir. Cook until onions are translucent.

To the saucepan, add the beef stock. Stir to combine. Cook over medium heat for 10 minutes.

Divide the soup evenly into bowls. Top each bowl with a slice of French bread and a sprinkle of the cheese mixture.

Place the bowls on a 17" X 12" baking sheet.

Set the oven to broil, and place the baking sheet in it. Broil for 3 minutes or until the cheese melts.

Enjoy!

SALADS

Mustard and Egg Potato Salad

Prep time: 1 hour and 5 minutes
Cooking time: 15 minutes
Serves 8–10

Ingredients

7 medium gold potatoes
2 tablespoons salt, divided
3 boiled eggs, divided
1 cup mayonnaise

½ cup dill relish
2 tablespoons yellow mustard
1 tablespoon black pepper
1 tablespoon paprika

Directions

Peel and dice the potatoes. Add to a large pot. Season with 1 tablespoon salt, and cover with water. Boil the potatoes on high heat for 15–20 minutes or until tender.

Peel the eggs. Set one aside. Dice the other two into small pieces.

Drain the potatoes, and let cool for 20 minutes.

In a large bowl, add the mayonnaise, relish, diced eggs, mustard, black pepper, and the remaining salt. Mix well.

Cut the remaining egg into quarters. Add to the top of the potato salad with a sprinkle of paprika for decoration.

Refrigerate for 30 minutes.

Enjoy!

Broccoli, Carrot, and Raisin Salad

Prep time: 15 minutes
Serves 4–6

This is a delicious, sweet salad. Substituting the raisins for dried cranberries makes it even sweeter. Try it both ways.

Ingredients

1 carrot

½ onion

½ red pepper

4 cups fresh broccoli florets

½ cup raisins

1 cup mayo

½ cup sugar

¼ teaspoon black pepper

Directions

Using a grater, shred the carrot. Dice the onion and pepper into small pieces.

In a large bowl, combine the broccoli, raisins, onion, red pepper, and carrot.

In a separate small bowl, whisk together the mayo and sugar. Season with black pepper, and whisk.

Pour salad dressing over vegetables and raisins. Combine well. Refrigerate for 1 hour.

Enjoy!

Seafood Pasta Salad

Prep time: 10 minutes
Cooking time: 25 minutes
Serves 10

This recipe is great for summer parties and catered events. It's very colorful, which gives it a great presentation. Substituting the imitation crab with one can of jumbo lump crabmeat elevates this recipe to an upscale dish.

Ingredients

½ gallon water

1 pound tricolored pasta

1 tablespoon salt

1 cup diced tomatoes

1 cup diced cucumbers

1 cup Italian dressing

½ cup shrimp, peeled, deveined, and cooked

½ cup chunk-style imitation crabmeat.

1 tablespoon Italian seasoning

2 teaspoons black pepper

Directions

Fill a large pot three-fourths the way full with water. Heat on high until the water starts to boil.

Add salt to the water and stir. Add the pasta to the water. Cook until al dente, stirring often.

Drain the pasta, and let cool for 10 minutes.

To a large bowl, add pasta, tomatoes, cucumbers, Italian dressing, shrimp, crabmeat, Italian seasoning, and black pepper. Mix well.

Refrigerate for 3 hours.

Enjoy!

Italian Pasta Salad

Prep time: 10 minutes
Cooking time: minutes
Serves 15

This recipe is great for summer parties. A cold dish is always nice in the summer heat.
It can also be served warm in the winter time as it is a versitile dish.

Ingredients

1 pound tricolored pasta, al dente
1 cup diced tomatoes
1 cup diced cucumbers
1 cup Italian dressing
½ cup black olives, sliced
¼ cup salami

¼ cup pepperoni
1 tablespoon Italian seasoning
1 tablespoon salt
1 teaspoon black pepper
1 cup shredded mozzarella cheese
¼ cup parmesan cheese

Directions

In a large bowl, combine pasta, tomatoes, cucumbers, Italian dressing, black olives, salami, and pepperoni. Season with Italian seasoning, salt, and black pepper. Mix well.
Refrigerate for 3 hours
Add the mozzarella and parmesan cheese. Stir well
Enjoy!

Cucumber Tomato Salad

Prep time: 15 minutes
Serves 6

This is a very easy and colorful recipe. It's great for picnics and catered events, because it's easy to make this dish in large quantities. If you are counting calories, you can use fat-free salad dressing.

Ingredients

1 pound yellow cherry tomatoes
1 pound red cherry tomatoes
2 cucumbers
1 red onion
1 cup Italian dressing
1 teaspoon salt
1 teaspoon black pepper

Directions

Slice both yellow and red cherry tomatoes in half. Thinly slice the cucumbers and onions.
In a large bowl, combine all ingredients. Stir well, and cover.
Refrigerate for 2 hours.
Mix well before serving, and enjoy!

MAIN DISHES

The Best Macaroni and Cheese Ever

Prep time: 20 minutes
Cooking time: 50 minutes
Serves 6–8

This is another of my signature dishes. The types of cheeses and milks used are what take it to the next level. This recipe truly lives up to its name.

Ingredients

½ gallon water

3 tablespoons salt, divided

1 (1-pound) box of elbow moodles

1 cup shredded gruyere cheese

1 cup shredded gouda cheese

1 cup shredded mozzarella cheese

1 cup shredded medium sharp cheese

1 cup shredded extra sharp cheese

2 12 ounce cans evaporated milk

1 cup whole milk

2 large eggs, beaten

½ teaspoon black pepper

cooking spray

1 stick unsalted butter

Directions

Preheat oven to 400 degrees

Bring water to a boil.

Add half the salt, and boil noodles according to the package's directions. Drain.

In a large bowl, combine all the cheeses. Measure out 1 cup of the cheese mixture, and set aside.

In a second lage bowl, combine evaporated milk, whole milk, eggs, pepper, the remaing salt, noodles, and the bowl of cheese. Combine well.

Spray a large baking dish with cooking spray. Add all the ingredients from the second large bowl and the butter. Cover with foil. Place in oven, and cook for 20 minutes.

Remove from oven. Stir, cover and place back in the oven for 25 additional minutes.

Remove the baking dish from the oven. Remove foil, and spread the remaining 1 cup of cheese on top.

Set the oven to broil. Place the baking dish in the oven, uncovered, and cook for 3–5 minutes or until browned. Enjoy!

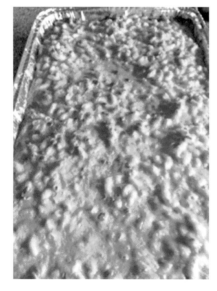

Chicken and Dressing

Prep time: 30 minutes
Cooking time: 1 hour and 15 minutes
Serves 4–6

Ingredients

2 8.5 ounce boxes corn bread mix
2 large chicken breast (skin on)
2 tablespoons black pepper, divided
4 ½ teaspoons salt, divided
3 eggs, divided
2 celery stalks
1 medium onion

1 green bell pepper
32 ounces chicken broth
3 tablespoons ground sage
1 teaspoon garlic powder
1 teaspoon onion powder
1 10.5 ounce can cream of mushroom soup

Directions

Preheat oven to 400 degrees.

Cook cornbread according to the package's directions, and set aside. Hard boil two eggs. Set aside.

Season chicken with garlic powder, onion powder, 1 tablespoon black pepper and 1 tablespoon salt . Place in a 4.8 quart baking dish, and bake for 45 minutes. Remove from the dish and set aside.

Finely chop the boiled eggs, celery, onion, and green bell pepper.

To a large pot, add the chicken broth, celery, onion, green bell pepper, sage, the remaining black pepper, and the remaining salt. Cook over medium heat for 15 minutes.

In a large bowl, crumble cornbread. Add the soup, raw egg, boiled eggs. Mix well.

Put cornbread mixture in the same 4.8 quart baking dish . Add broth mixture, stirring continuously. It should be very moist but not wet.

Place chicken breasts in the casserole dish, on top, and bake for 30 minutes.

Enjoy!

Jambalaya

Prep time: 30 minutes
Cooking time: 1 hour and 20 minutes
Serves 8–10

This is a great dish to cook in a large quantity.

Ingredients

1 large boneless, skinless chicken breast
1 teaspoon seasoning salt
1 teaspoon Italian seasoning
1 teaspoon garlic powder
1 teaspoon salt
1 teaspoon black pepper
1 teaspoon creole seasoning
½ teaspoon red pepper flakes
4 tablespoons vegetable oil, divided
3 smoked sausages
2 celery stalks

1 large onion
1 large green bell pepper
2 tablespoons minced garlic
32 ounces chicken broth
3 cups white rice
1 15 ounce can tomato sauce
1 10 ounce can diced tomatoes with green chilies
¼ cup fresh parsley, divided
2 4 ounce cans sliced mushrooms
1 pound cooked shrimp

Directions

Preheat oven to 400 degrees.

Cut chicken into small pieces.

In a small bowl, combine the seasoning salt, Italian seasoning, garlic powder, salt, black pepper, creole seasoning, and red pepper flakes.

Season the chicken with half the seasoning mixture.

Heat 2 tablespoons oil in a medium skillet. Add chicken, and sauté for 3 minutes on each side. Set aside.

Slice sausages into ¼-inch thick rounds.

Dice the celery, onion, and green bell pepper. Set aside.

Heat the remaining oil in a second large skillet on high. Add the sausage, celery, onion, green bell pepper, and minced garlic. Reduce heat to medium, and cook for 5 minutes.

In a large casserole dish, combine the chicken broth, rice, tomato sauce, diced tomatoes, the remaining spice mixture, half the parsley, and the sausage mixture. Stir well. Cover and place in the oven. Cook for 45 minutes.

Remove the casserole dish from the oven, and stir. Add the mushrooms, cooked chicken, and shrimp. Stir well, and place back in the oven. Cook for an additional 35 minutes.

Remove from oven, and garnish with the remaining parsley.

Enjoy!

Sausages, Potatoes, and Peppers

Prep time: 5 minutes
Cooking time:45 minutes
Serves 4

Ingredients

3 large red potatoes

2 smoked sausage

1 green bell pepper

1 onion

2 tablespoons olive oil

2 tablespoons minced garlic

1 teaspoon salt

1 teaspoon black pepper

1 teaspoon creole seasoning

Directions

Preheat oven to 375 degrees.

Wash and slice the potatoes into approximately 1/4-inch thick slices Slice the sausages into approximately 1/4-inch thick rounds. Slice the green bell pepper and onion into slivers.

To a large bowl, add the potatoes, bell pepper, onion, olive oil, minced garlic, salt, black pepper, and creole seasoning. Combine well, and transfer to a medium size 8' X 8" baking dish. Spread sausages on top. Cover and place in oven. Bake for 45 minutes.

Remove from oven. Stir well.

Enjoy!

Spicy Chili

Prep time: 10 minutes
Cooking time: 30 minutes
Serves 6

Ingredients

1 pound ground beef
2 tablespoons chili powder, divided
2 tablespoons salt, divided
2 teaspoons black pepper, divided
2 teaspoons garlic powder, divided

1 (30-ounce) can hot chili beans
30 ounces water
1 cup chunky medium salsa
1 teaspoon cumin

Directions

Heat a large skillet over medium heat. Add ground beef. Season with 1 tablespoon chili powder, 1 tablespoon salt, 1 teaspoon black pepper, and 1 teaspoon garlic powder. Cook until meat is brown.

Drain the excess grease from the skillet.

To a large pot, add the chili beans, water, salsa, and ground beef. Season with the cumin, the remaining 1 tablespoon chili powder, 1 tablespoon salt, 1 teaspoon black pepper, and 1 teaspoon garlic powder. Stir well. Simmer for 20 minutes.

Once chili is done, serve in bowls. It can be topped with cheese, sour cream, and green onions.

Enjoy!

Spinach, Egg, and Cheese Bake

Prep time: 15 minutes
Cooking time: 35 minutes
Serves 6

Enjoy this dish during breakfast, lunch, or dinner. It's also great to serve at a catered brunch.

Ingredients

1 tablespoon vegetable oil
¼ cup diced onions
2 pounds baby spinach
2 teaspoons salt, divided
2 teaspoons black pepper, divided

8 eggs
½ cup mozzarella cheese, shredded
¼ cup medium cheddar cheese, shredded
cooking spray

Directions

Preheat the oven to 375 degrees.

Heat oil in a large skillet over high heat. Add the onions. Cook for 1 minute.

Add a handful of the spinach to the skillet. Mix well. Repeat until all spinach has been added. Season with 1 teaspoon of salt and 1 teaspoon of black pepper. Mix well. Set aside to cool.

In a small bowl, whisk eggs with the remaining 1 teaspoon salt and 1 teaspoon black pepper. Add the cheese. Stir in the cooled spinach.

Spray a 9" X 13" baking dish with the cooking oil. Pour the in spinach and egg mixture. Place in the oven, and bake for 35 minutes.

Enjoy!

Breakfast Casserole

Prep time:15 minutes
Cooking time: 35 minutes
Serves 6

If you are serving a large crowd, this will be the perfect breakfast dish. It's also amazing as brunch.
If you would like, you can add red or green bell peppers, mushrooms, or cooked spinach.

Ingredients

1 onion

1 loaf sourdough bread, sliced

1 (16-ounce) tube breakfast sausage

8 eggs

8 ounces milk

2 teaspoons salt

2 teaspoons black pepper, divided

1 teaspoon garlic powder

1 tablespoon butter

16 ounces hash browns

2 cups shredded cheddar cheese, divided

Directions

Dice the onion. Cut the bread into 1" cubes.

In a large skillet on high heat, cook the sausage and onions for 5 minutes. Set aside.

In a large bowl, scramble the eggs. Add milk. Season with the salt, 1 teaspoon black pepper, and garlic powder.

Butter a 9" X 13" casserole dish . Line with the bread. Add the hash browns. Season with 1 teaspoon black pepper .

Sprinkle half the cheese on top. Add the sausage and onion mixture. Pour the eggs on top.

Cover the casserole dish, and refrigerate overnight.

The next day, preheat the oven to 400 degrees.

Uncover the casserole dish, and add the remining cheese. Place in oven. Bake for 35 minutes

Enjoy!

VEGETABLES

Smothered Cabbage

Prep time: 10 minutes
Cooking time:10 minutes
Serves 6

The is one of the best and healthiest ways to eat cabbage, and tasty too.

Ingredients

1 head cabbage

1 yellow onion

1 green bell pepper

2 tablespoons vegetable oil

2 tablespoons minced garlic

½ cup water

2 teaspoons creole seasoning

2 teaspoons salt

2 teaspoons black pepper

½ teaspoon red pepper flakes

Directions

Slice the cabbage into 1-inch squares. Place in a colander, and rinse well. Drain.

Dice the onion and pepper into medium-sized chunks.

In a large skillet, heat oil over medium heat for 2 minutes. Add the onions and peppers. Sauté for 3 minutes.

Add the cabbage and garlic to the skillet. Cook for 3 minutes, stirring often.

To the skillet, add the water. Season with creole seasoning, salt, black pepper, and red pepper flakes. Stir well, and cover. Cook for an additional 5 minutes.

Enjoy!

Stuffed Green Bell Peppers

Prep time: 15 minutes
Cooking time: 20 minutes
Serves 6

Ingredients

2 15 ounce cans tomato sauce

1 ounce can diced tomatoes with green chilies

2 teaspoons salt, divided

2 teaspoons black pepper, divided

1 teaspoon garlic powder

4 green bell peppers, divided

1 onion

1 pound ground beef

1 teaspoon minced garlic

2 cups cooked rice

Directions

Preheat oven to 350 degrees.

To a medium pot, add the tomato sauce and diced tomatoes. Season with 1 teaspoon salt, 1 teaspoon black pepper, and the garlic powder. Cook on medium heat for 3 minutes. Set aside.

Dice one of the green peppers and the onion. Sauté in a medium pan for 5 minutes on medium heat. Add the ground beef and minced garlic. Season with the remaining 1 teaspoon salt and 1 teaspoon black pepper. Cook until browned.

In a large bowl, combine the beef mixture and the rice. Mix well.

Cut the tops off the remaining three peppers. Remove the seeds. Place the peppers in a pot of boiling water for 2 minutes.

Remove the peppers from the pot, and rinse in ice water. Set aside.

Spread half the tomato mixture over the bottom of a 9" X 13" baking dish .

Using an ice cream scooper, fill the peppers with the beef and rice mixture. Place the stuffed peppers in the baking dish. Add 2 tablespoons of the tomato mixture to the top of each pepper. Cover the baking dish with foil, and place in the oven. Bake for 20 minutes.

Enjoy!

Southern-Fried Corn

Prep time:15 minutes
Cooking time: 20 minutes
Serves 6

Ingredients

6 slices bacon

1 stick butter

1 medium onion, diced

1 large green bell pepper, diced

3 (15.25-ounce) cans whole kernel corn

2 teaspoons salt

1 teaspoon black pepper

Directions

In a large skillet on medium heat, cook the bacon for 4 minutes on each side.

Remove the bacon from the skillet. Cut into small pieces, and set aside.

To the skillet with the bacon grease, add the butter, onion, and bell pepper.Sauté on medium heat until soft.

Add the corn and bacon to the skillet. Mix well. Season with the salt and pepper. Stir well. Cook over medium heat for 10 minutes.

Enjoy!

Vegetable Medley

Prep time: 20 minutes
Cook: time 10 minutes
Serves 4–6

Who says eating healthy has to taste bad? Not if you are enjoying this recipe. It's very healthy and full of tasty flavors. The colorful presentation adds a nice touch as well.

Ingredients

1 large zucchini

1 yellow squash

1 medium onion

1 green bell pepper

1 red bell pepper

2 tablespoons olive oil

2 teaspoons salt

½ teaspoon black pepper

½ teaspoon garlic powder

Directions

Slice the zucchini and squash into ¼-inch circles. Slice the onion and bell peppers into thin strips.

In a large skillet, heat olive oil on medium heat. Add the zucchini, squash, onion, and bell peppers. Season with the salt, black pepper, and garlic powder. Combine well. Cover the skillet, and continue to cook over medium heat for ten minutes.

Enjoy!

Roasted Asparagus

Prep time: 10 minutes
Cooking time: 10 minutes
Serves 4

When looking for a classy vegetable for a special dinner party, you can't go wrong with these asparagus. It's a restaurant-quality dish with such an easy recipe.

Ingredients

1 pound fresh asparagus

2 tablespoons olive oil

1 tablespoon minced garlic

1 teaspoon salt

1 teaspoon black pepper

Directions

Preheat oven to 400 degrees.

Cut 1 inch off the flat end of each asparagus.

In a small bowl, combine the olive oil and garlic. Mix well.

On a 7" X 12" baking sheet, spread out the asparagus. Brush the oil mixture over each asparagus. Sprinkle with the salt and pepper.

Place the baking sheet in the oven, and roast for 10 minutes.

Enjoy!

Fried Green Tomatoes

Prep time: 10 minutes
Cooking time: 10 minutes
Serves 4

Fried Green Tomatoes are a delicious southern delicacy. With this recipe, everyone will think you have real southern roots.

Ingredients

1 cup flour
3 eggs
1 cup milk
1 cup corn meal
1 cup seasoned bread crumbs
1 cup panko bread crumbs
1 teaspoon salt

1 teaspoon black pepper
1 teaspoon cayenne pepper
1 teaspoon garlic powder
1 teaspoon onion powder
2 green tomatoes
2 tablespoons olive oil

Directions

To a shallow bowl, add the flour.

In a second shallow bowl, scramble the eggs, and add the milk. Whisk well.

In a third shallow bowl, combine the cornmeal, seasoned bread crumbs, and panko bread crumbs.

In a fourth shallow bowl, add the salt, black pepper, cayenne pepper, garlic powder, and onion powder. Mix well. Add half the mixture to the third bowl, and mix.

Wash the tomatoes. Using a serrated knife, slice into rounds that are 0.25–0.5 inch thick. Place slices on a sheet of paper towel to dry.

Sprinkle the remaining half of the seasoning mixture on top of tomatoes.

In a large skillet, heat the oil to 350 degrees.

Dip a tomato slice into the flour. Shake off any excess. Lightly coat with the egg mixture. Dip into the bread crumb mixture, shaking off any excess. Place on a piece of parchment paper. Repeat until all tomatoes are coated.

Place the tomatoes in the skillet, and cook for approximately 2 minutes on each side or until golden brown.

Place the cooked tomatoes on a sheet of paper towel to remove excess oil.

Enjoy!

Creamed Spinach and Cheese

Prep time: 5 minutes
Cooking time: 10 minutes
Serves 4

Ingredients

½ onion
2 tablespoons olive oil
3 pounds fresh spinach
1 cup heavy whipping cream

¼ cup parmesan cheese
2 slices provolone cheese
1 teaspoon salt
½ teaspoon black pepper

Directions

Dice the onion into small pieces.

Add the oil to a medium size pan. Heat over medium heat. Add the spinach and onions. Sauté for approximately 5 minutes.

Drain the spinach and return it to the pan. Add the heavy whipping cream, parmesan cheese, and provolone. Season with the salt and black pepper. Stir well, and cook for 5 minutes.

Enjoy!

PASTA

Pasta à Lavonne

Prep time: 15 minutes
Cooking time: 30 minutes
Serves 13

This is my all-time favorite signature dish. It's a creamy pasta dish that is extremely flavorful, colorful, and filled with just enough seafood. If you are a pasta lover, a seafood lover, or a Cajun food lover, this dish is sure to delight your pallet.

Ingredients

1 large onion
1 red bell pepper
1 green bell pepper
1 orange bell pepper
1 yellow bell pepper
2 tablespoons olive oil
16 ounces fettuccini
½ stick unsalted butter
1 pound shrimp, deveined and cooked
1 pound crawfish tails

2 teaspoons cajun seasoning
2 teaspoons salt
2 teaspoons black pepper
2 cups heavy whipping cream
1 cup pesto
1 cup sliced mushrooms
1 cup cherry tomatoes
2 tablespoons parmesan cheese
1 tablespoon mince garlic

Directions

Julienne the onion and the red, green, orange, and yellow bell peppers into thin strips.

In a medium skillet, heat the olive oil over medium heat. Add the onion and peppers, and sauté until soft. Set aside.

Cook the pasta according to the package's directions, and drain.

In a large skillet, melt the butter over medium heat. Add the shrimp and crawfish. Sauté for 3 minutes.

Add the peppers, garlic and onions to the skillet with the shrimp and crawfish. Season with the cajun seasoning, salt, and black pepper. Mix well.

Add the heavy whipping cream and pesto to the shrimp mixture. Stir thoroughly. Then add the mushrooms and tomatoes. Mix well.

Add the cooked pasta to the shrimp mixture, and combine. Cook for an additional 10 minutes.

Top with parmesan cheese, and enjoy.

Creamy Chicken, Mushroom, and Broccoli Pasta

Prep time: 5 minutes
Cooking time: 25 minutes
Serves 4–6

*This will definetly become one of your favorite go to casseroles when looking
for something quick, easy and delicious to eat during the week.*

Ingredients

1 pound penne

1 rotisserie chicken

8 ounces fresh button mushrooms

2 10.5 ounce cans cream of chicken soup

32 ounces heavy whipping cream

2 teaspoons black pepper

1 teaspoon salt

1 cup fresh broccoli florets

Directions

In a large pot, cook the pasta according to the package's directions. Drain and put back into the large pot.

Remove the bones from the chicken, and shred the meat.

Clean and slice the mushrooms.

Heat a medium pan over medium heat. Add the chicken soup. Whisk in the heavy whipping cream. Add the chicken and mushrooms. Season with the black pepper and salt. Mix well.

Rough chop the broccoli, and add to the pot. Turn the heat down to low, and cook for 15 minutes.

Pour the cream mixture over the pasta, and combine well. Add more salt if needed.

Enjoy!

Swedish Meatballs with Vegetables and Noodles

Prep time: 5 minutes
Cooking time: 25 minutes
Serves 4–6

This is comfort food at its best. The sauce is flavorful and creamy. Your entire family will love this meal. The recipe can be passed down to future generations.

Ingredients

1 pound egg noodles
1 onion
1 red bell pepper
1 orange bell pepper
1 tablespoon olive oil
1 teaspoon minced garlic
1 pound frozen meatballs
2 cups fresh broccoli florets
15 ounces Swedish meatball sauce [4]
2 teaspoons salt
2 teaspoons black pepper

Directions

Preheat oven to 400 degrees.

In a large pot, cook the pasta according to the package's directions. Drain the pasta, saving the water. Set both aside.

Slice the onion and the red and orange bell peppers.

Heat a skillet over medium heat. Add the oil, onion, and peppers. Sauté for 3 minutes. Then add the minced garlic, and stir well.

In a large baking dish, combine the meatballs and broccoli. Add the pepper and onion mixture and the meatball sauce. Season with salt and black pepper. Mix well.

To the baking dish, add the pasta and 1 cup pasta water. Stir to combine.

Cover the baking dish, and put in the oven. Bake for 20 minutes.

Enjoy!

---

[4]   See page 119 for recipe.

Shrimp Pasta in a Exquisite Sauce

Prep time: 10 minutes
Cooking time: 15 minutes
Serves 4

*This is a romantic dish full of Shrimp and Pasta in a Garlicky, Tomatoe and white Wine Sauce.
A robust flavor that's sure to please.*

Ingredients

8 ounces angel-hair pasta

2 tablespoons olive oil

1 green bell pepper, diced

½ onion, diced

2 cloves garlic, chopped

1 (8-ounce) can tomato paste

1 (10-ounce) can diced tomatoes with green chilies

16 ounces white wine

¼ cup chopped Parsley

1 teaspoon salt

1 teaspoon black pepper

1 pound shrimp, deveined and cooked

Directions

Prepare the pasta according to the package's directions, and set aside.

In a large skillet, heat olive oil over medium heat. Add the diced green bell pepper and onion. Cook until translucent, stirring continuously.

Add the chopped garlic and tomato paste to the skillet. Stir for 1 minute. Then add the canned tomatoes, and stir.

Add the white wine to the skillet. Season with the parsley, salt, and black pepper.

Add the shrimp and pasta to the skillet. Mix well.

Enjoy!

Penne Bolognese

Prep time: 10 minutes
Cooking time: 45 minutes
Serves 8–10

When cooking for a large crowd, this is a delicious pasta dish that will win the hearts of everyone.

Ingredients

1 pound ground beef

2 teaspoons ground parsley, divided

2 teaspoons garlic powder

1 teaspoon black pepper

1 teaspoon Italian seasoning

1 teaspoon basil

1 28 oz jar thick and chunky marinara sauce

¼ cup medium salsa

½ gallon water

1 pound penne

2 tablespoons salt

1 cup parmesan cheese

Directions

To a large pot, add the ground beef. Season with half the ground parsley, the garlic powder, black pepper, Italian seasoning, and basil. Cook over medium heat for approximately 5 minutes or until beef is brown, stirring occasionally.

Add the marinara sauce and salsa to the pot. Stir well, and cook for an additional 5 minutes.

Refrigerate sauce overnight.

The next day, remove the sauce from the refrigerator. Preheat oven to 350 degrees.

To a second large pot, add water. Bring to a boil. Add pasta and salt. Cook until al dente (approx 6 minutes), stirring often.

Drain the pasta, saving 1 cup water.

To a large roasting pan, add the pasta, half the sauce, and the water. Combine well. Add more sauce if needed.[5]

Cover the pan, and place in the oven for 30 minutes.

Remove pan from the oven, and uncover. Stir. Garnish with the remaining parsley.

Divide pasta into bowls, and top with the parmesan cheese.

Enjoy!

---

[5] If any sauce remains, place in a freezer bag, and freeze.

Grilled Shrimp Scampi à Lavonne

Prep time: 10 minutes
Cooking time: 10 minutes
Serves 4

This recipe is a shrimp lover's dream.

Ingredients

1 pound angel-hair pasta

1 red onion

1 orange bell pepper

1 red bell pepper

3 tablespoons olive oil, divided

2 tablespoons minced garlic

1 stick butter

2 cups heavy whipping cream

1 (4-ounce) can sliced mushrooms

2 tablespoons parmesan cheese

1 ½ teaspoons salt

1 teaspoon black pepper

1 pound shrimp, peeled, deveined, and cooked

1 tablespoon garlic powder

Directions

Cook the pasta according to the package's directions. Drain and set aside.

Julienne the onion and orange and red bell peppers.

In a large skillet, heat 2 tablespoons olive oil over medium heat. Add the onion and bell peppers. Sauté for 3 minutes.

Add the garlic to the onion and bell peppers, and stir. Cook for 1 minute. Then add the butter. Cook until melted, stirring continuously.

To the skillet, add the cream, mushrooms, and parmesan cheese. Season with salt and black pepper.

Add the pasta to the sauce, and stir to combine.

Season the shrimp with the garlic powder.

In a separate medium skillet, heat the remaining 1 tablespoon olive oil for one minute on medium heat. Cook the shrimp for 1 minute on each side.

Add shrimp to the pasta mixture. Stir well, and remove from heat.

Enjoy!

Cajun Chicken Pasta

Prep time: 15 minutes
Cooking time: 20 minutes
Serves 4–6

This is one of my spicy dishes. If you like spice, you will love this recipe.

Ingredients

16 ounces penne

1 large red bell pepper

2 tablespoons olive oil

2 tablespoons cajun seasoning, divided

2 tablespoons minced garlic

2 teaspoons salt

2 teaspoons black pepper

2 boneless skinless chicken breasts

3 tablespoons vegetable oil

4 cups shredded Mexican cheese blend

2 cups heavy whipping cream

Directions

Boil pasta according to the package's directions.

Thinly slice the red bell pepper.

Heat the olive oil in a large skillet on medium heat. Add the red bell pepper, 1 teaspoon cajun seasoning, the minced garlic, the salt, and the black pepper. Sauté for 5 minutes.

Dice the chicken. Season with 1 tablespoon cajun seasoning.

In a separate large skillet, heat the vegetable oil over high heat. Add the chicken, and cook for 5 minutes.

In a medium saucepan, combine the cheese, heavy whipping cream, and the remaining 2 teaspoons cajun seasoning. Whisk and simmer for 5 minutes or until creamy.

Add the peppers, pasta, and chicken to the cheese sauce. Stir well.

Enjoy!

Three-Cheese Mostaccioli

Prep time: 25 minutes
Cooking time: 15 minutes
Serves 4

Ingredients

1 pound penne

2 teaspoons parsley

2 teaspoons basil

2 teaspoons oregano

2 teaspoons salt

2 teaspoons black pepper

1 pound ground beef

2 (10-ounce) can marinara sauce

½ cup grated mozzarella cheese

½ cup grated mild cheddar cheese

2 tablespoons grated parmesan cheese

Directions

Preheat oven to 375 degrees.

In a large pot, cook the pasta according to the package's directions. Drain and set aside.

In a small bowl, combine the parsley, basil, oregano, salt, and black pepper.

To a large skillet, add the ground beef and half the seasoning mixture. Cook on medium until meat is brown.

Drain the excess grease from the skillet. Combine the marinara sauce with the ground beef. Stir well. Season with the other half of the seasoning mixture. Mix and cook over low heat for 5 minutes.

Line the bottom of a large baking dish with half the sauce. Add the pasta. Top with the remaining sauce. Mix well. Sprinkle the mozzarella cheese, cheddar cheese, and parmesan cheese on top of the pasta. Place the baking dish in the oven. Bake for 15 minutes.

Enjoy!

Five-Cheese Tortellini with Virgin Vodka Sauce

Prep time: 5 minutes
Cooking time: 15 minutes
Serves 4

Vodka sauce is delicious with pasta; however, some people don't use liquor when cooking. So I invented the virgin vodka sauce. It tastes just as amazing as the one with vodka, and your kids can enjoy it too.

Ingredients

12 ounces five-cheese tortellini

1 (10-ounce) can tomato Sauce

1 (10-ounce) can diced tomatoes with green chilies

1 (4-ounce) can sliced mushrooms

1 cup heavy whipping cream

2 tablespoons parmesan cheese

1 teaspoon salt

1 teaspoon black pepper

1 teaspoon Italian seasoning

Directions

In a large pot, cook the tortellini according to the package's directions. Drain and set aside.

To a medium pot, add the tomato sauce, tomatoes, and mushrooms. Stir well. Add the heavy whipping cream and parmesan cheese. Season with the salt, black pepper, and Italian seasoning. Combine well. Heat on medium for 5 minutes.

Add the sauce to the pasta. Mix well.

Enjoy!

SIDE DISHES

Pickled Red Onions

Prep time: 5 minutes
Cooking time: 3 minutes
Serves 8–10

Ingredients
2 cups white vinegar
⅓ cup sugar
1 teaspoon salt
2 red onions

Directions
To a small pot, add the vinegar, sugar, and salt. Stir well, and bring to a boil.
Thinly slice the onions.
Place the onions in a medium container that has a lid. Pour the liquid over the onions, making sure all onions are covered.
Place a lid on container, and let sit for 1 hour.
Refrigerate container overnight before using.
Enjoy!

Scalloped Potatoes

Prep time: 30 minutes
Cooking time: 75 minutes
Serves 8-10

Ingredients

½ stick butter

1 large onion, thinly sliced

½ cup flour

32 ounces chicken or vegetable broth

3 cups shredded cheddar cheese, divided

3 cups shredded Mexican four-cheese blend, divided

½ cup parmesan cheese

¼ cup evaporated milk

2 tablespoons garlic powder

2 tablespoons black pepper

2 tablespoons kosher salt

6 large potatoes, thinly sliced

2 cups sour cream

¼ cup half-and-half

Directions

Preheat oven to 400 degrees. Spray a 9X13 pan with nonstick cooking spray.

In a medium skillet, melt the butter over medium heat. Add the onion slices. Sauté until they are translucent.

Add the flour to the onions, stirring constantly. Then add broth, and stir.

In a small bowl, combine 1 cup cheddar cheese and 1 cup Mexican four-cheese blend. Set aside

In medium bowl, combine the remaining 2 cups cheddar cheese, the remaining 2 cups Mexican four-cheese blend, and the Parmesan cheese. Mix well. Add to the skillet, stirring constantly.

Add the half-and-half and evaporated milk to the skillet while stirring. Season with 1 tablespoon garlic powder, 1 tablespoon black pepper, and 1 tablespoon kosher salt. Remove from heat, and set aside.

Add a third of the potatoes to the bottom of the greased pan. Lightly coat with sour cream. Season with a pinch each of salt, pepper, and garlic powder. Layer a third of the cheese sauce and a third of the shredded cheese mixture. Repeat two more times, ending with the shredded cheese mixture.

Cover the pan with foil, and put in the oven. Cook for 75 minutes.

Remove pan from oven. Poke the potatoes with a fork to see if they are soft. If not, cook for an additional 15 minutes.

Let sit for 15 minutes to become firm before serving.

Enjoy!

Baked Beans with Ground Beef and Pineapples

Prep time: 15 minutes
Cooking time: 45 minutes
Serves 12

This recipe serves a lot of people and is good for leftovers. It can be cut in half if necessary.

Ingredients

1 large onion
1 green bell pepper
2 tablespoons vegetable oil
1 pound ground beef
1 teaspoon black pepper

1 teaspoon paprika
1 10# can baked beans
1 cup brown sugar
¾ cup pineapple tidbits, drained
2 tablespoons honey mustard

Directions

Preheat oven to 375 degrees.

Finely dice the onion and green bell pepper.

In a large skillet, on medium heat, heat the oil. Add the onion and green bell pepper. Cook until soft.

To a separate large skillet, add the ground beef, black pepper, and paprika. Cook 5 minutes, and then drain.

In a large baking dish, combine the ground beef, onion, bell pepper, beans, sugar, pinapple tidbits, and mustard. Stir until all the ingredients are thoroughly combined.

Cover the baking dish, and place in the oven. Bake for 45 minutes.

Remove from the oven.

Enjoy!

Garlic-Roasted Potatoes

Prep time: 10 minutes
Cooking time: 10 minutes
Serves 4–6

Ingredients

4 red potatoes
1 red onion
1 red bell pepper
1 green bell pepper
3 tablespoons olive oil
2 tablespoons minced garlic
1 ½ teaspoons salt
1 teaspoon black pepper

Directions

Preheat oven to 400 degrees.

Cut the potatoes into large chunks. Slice the onions. Julienne the red and green bell peppers.

To a large casserole dish, add the potatoes, onion, bell peppers, olive oil, garlic, salt, and black pepper. Combine well.

Cover the casserole dish, and place in the oven. Bake for 45 minutes.

To test for doneness, poke potatoes with a fork. If they are not soft, cook for an additional 15 minutes.

Enjoy!

Hot Water Cornbread

Prep time: 15 minutes
Cooking time: 30minutes
Serves 13

Ingredients

4 cups yellow cornmeal

1 cup all-purpose flour

2 teaspoons salt

4 ¾ cups water, boiling

½ stick butter, melted

¼ cup vegetable oil

Directions

In a large bowl, whisk together cornmeal, flour, and salt. Add hot water and butter. Stir for 2 minutes.

Heat oil in a skillet on high heat .

Place (3) at a time 4 tablespoonfuls of mixture in the hot oil. Cook for 4–5 minutes on each side. Remove from skillet, and place on a plate lined with paper towels. Repeat until mixture is gone.

Enjoy!

DESSERTS

Mexican Fried Ice Cream

Prep time: 5 minutes
Cooking time: 5 minutes
Serves 6

Ingredients

1 cup cornflakes
½ gallon vanilla ice cream
1 cup granulated sugar
1 teaspoon cinnamon
4 cup vegetable oil
3 ounces strawberry syrup or chocolate syrup

Directions

In a large bowl, crush the cornflakes.

Using an ice cream scooper, place one scoop of ice cream in the bowl. Coat with cornflakes, making sure the flakes are patted down and the entire ball is covered. Place on a 17 X 12" baking sheet . Repeat until ice cream is gone.

Cover the baking sheet with plastic wrap, and place in the freezer overnight.

The next day, combine sugar and cinnamon in a separate medium bowl .

In a Dutch oven or large pot, on high heat, heat the oil.

Place the ice cream balls in the oil, and roll them around for 3 seconds. Then remove the balls from the oil.

Roll the ice cream balls in the cinnamon sugar mixture.

Serve them plain, or drizzle them with strawberry syrup or chocolate syrup.

Enjoy!

Sweet Potato Pie

Prep time: 35 minutes
Cooking time: 20 minutes
Serves 6

No Thanksgiving dinner is complete without one of these pies. Make them for all your holidays and Sunday dinners. Your family will thank you.

Ingredients

2 large sweet potatoes
1 stick butter, melted
2 cups of sugar
1 cup of milk
2 eggs

1 ½ teaspoons ground cinnamon
1 teaspoon vanilla extract
¼ teaspoon nutmeg
2 frozen pie crusts, in pans

Directions

Preheat the oven to 375 degrees.

Wash and peel the potatoes. Cut into large chunks.

In a large pot, boil the sweet potatoes until soft. Drain the water.

To a large bowl, add the potatoes, butter, sugar, milk, eggs, ground cinnamon, vanilla extract, and nutmeg. Using a hand mixer, blend until the potatoes are creamy.

Add the mixture from the bowl to the pie shells. Smooth out the top.

Bake pies in the oven for 20 minutes.

Remove from the oven, and cool for 15 minutes.

Enjoy!

Sweet and Creamy Homemade Whipped Cream

Prep time: 2 minutes
Makes 2 cups

Never worry about not having a dessert topping in the house again. Make your own with this extremely easy recipe. If you like it very sweet, double the amount of sugar. It goes well with any dessert.

Ingredients
2 cups heavy whipping cream
¼ cup powdered sugar
½ teaspoon vanilla extract

Directions
Add all ingredients to a large, cold bowl .
Using a hand mixer, mix on high, until the cream is stiff.
Enjoy!

Bread Pudding with Rum Sauce

Prep time: 1 hour
Cooking time: 55 minutes
Serves 4

This is a very rich and tasty dessert. The recipe is easily made with ingredients you would usually have in the house, so you can cook it all the time.

Ingredients
4 cups stale French bread
4 large eggs
1 cup milk
1 cup heavy whipping cream
¾ cup sugar
1 ounce butter
1 teaspoon cinnamon
1 teaspoon vanilla extract
1 cup rum sauce [6]

Directions
Preheat oven to 350 degrees. Butter an 8" X 8" casserole dish.

Cut the bread into 1-inch cubes. Add to the casserole dish.

Beat the eggs in a large bowl. Add the milk, heavy whipping cream, sugar, butter, cinnamon, and vanilla extract. Whisk well.

Pour the mixture from the bowl into a medium pot, and cook on low for 10 minutes.

Let the mixture cool for 15 minutes.

Pour the mixture over the bread. Let the bread soak in the mixture for 30 minutes.

Place the casserole dish in the oven. Bake for 40 minutes.

Take the casserole dish out of the oven. Divide pudding into four bowls. Pour the rum sauce over each. Enjoy!

---

[6]   See page 126 for recipe.

Strawberry Syrup

Prep time: 10 minutes
Cooking time: 45 minutes
Serves 4–6

Ingredients

1 pound fresh strawberries
1 cup sugar
½ lemon

Directions

Wash the strawberries, and slice in half.

To a medium saucepan, add strawberries and sugar. Squeeze the juice from the lemon on top. Combine well.

Bring the saucepan to a boil.[7] Reduce heat to medium, and cook for 30 minutes.

Let sauce cool.

Serve over ice cream, waffles, pancakes, poundcake, and more.

Enjoy!

---

[7] If you want your syrup to be thick, whisk together 1 tablespoon cornstarch and 2 tablespoons water. Add to the saucepan after it starts to boil.

Pineapple Carrot Cake

Prep time: 30 minutes
Cooking time: 40 minutes
Serves 8–10

*This is my favorite dessert, and of course, it is one of my signature dishes.
The pineapples are what make it so moist and tasty.*

Ingredients
Cake

2 cups and 3 tablespoon all-purpose flour, divided

2 cups sugar

2 teaspoons baking soda

2 teaspoons ground cinnamon

1 teaspoon salt

4 eggs

1-½ cup vegetable oil

3 cups grated carrot

2 cups pecans, chopped

¼ cup crushed pineapples, drained

Frosting

2 (8-ounce) packages cream cheese, room temperature

1 (16-ounce) bag powdered sugar

1 stick salted butter, room temperature

1 teaspoon vanilla extract

Directions
For the Cake

Preheat oven to 350 degrees. Grease three 9-inch round pans Dust the bottoms with 1 teaspoon of flour each. Line the bottom with parchment paper.

In a large bowl, combine the remaining 2 cups flour with the sugar, baking soda, cinnamon and salt. Add the eggs and vegetable oil. Using a hand mixer, blend until thoroughly combined.

Add the carrots, pecans, and pineapples to the bowl .Stir.

Pour the batter from the bowl into (3) 8" pans. Scrape the sides of the bowl to get all of the batter.

Place the pans in the oven. Bake for 40 minutes or until done.[8]

Remove the cakes from the pans and allow to cool completely before frosting.

For the Frosting

To a medium bowl, add cream cheese, powdered sugar, butter, and vanilla extract. Using a hand mixer, beat until fluffy.

Once the cakes have cooled, frost and stack them.

Enjoy!

---

[8]   To test for doneness, poke the cakes with a toothpick. If the toothpick comes out clean, the cake is done.

Peachy Hawaiian French Toast

Prep time: 10 minutes
Cooking time: 10 minutes
Serves 3–4

This recipe can be used for dessert or breakfast. Try it for both.

Ingredients

3 fresh peaches
2 sticks unsalted butter, divided
½ cup brown sugar
½ cup granulated sugar
2 teaspoons nutmeg, divided
2 teaspoons cinnamon, divided
2 tablespoons water
1 tablespoons cornstarch
1 ½ cups milk
4 eggs
2 teaspoons vanilla extract, divided
6–8 Hawaiian rolls, presliced
¼ cup powdered sugar
3 cups whipped cream [9]

Directions

Peel, wash, and slice the peaches.

Melt 1 stick of butter in a large skillet over medium heat.

To the skillet, add the peaches, brown sugar, and granulated sugar. Season with 1 teaspoon nutmeg, 1 teaspoon vanilla and 1 teaspoon cinnamon. Stir well. Simmer for 5 minutes.

Whisk water and cornstarch together in a bowl to create a slurry. Add to the skillet with the peach mixture. Stir until thick.

To a medium bowl, add the milk and eggs. Season with 1 teaspoon vanilla extract, the remaining 1 teaspoon cinnamon, and the remaining 1 teaspoon nutmeg. Whisk well.

In a second skillet, melt the remaining stick of butter.

Dip the bread in the milk mixture, making sure it is completely coated. Place the rolls in the skillet with the melted butter. Cook for 1 minute on each.

Place the cooked bread on a plate. Top with the peach mixture, powdered sugar, and whipped cream.

Enjoy!

---

[9]   See page 114 for recipe.

Peach Cobbler

Prep time: 30 minutes
Cooking time: 35 minutes
Serves 8–10

Ingredients

1 (29-ounce) can sliced peaches

¾ cup sugar

½ stick salted butter

1 teaspoon vanilla extract

½ teaspoon ground cinnamon

½ teaspoon nutmeg

2 refrigerated pie crusts, divided

¼ cup all-purpose flour

Directions

Preheat oven to 350 degrees.

To a medium pot, add the peaches and juice from the can. Add the sugar, butter, vanilla extract, cinnamon, and nutmeg. Stir well, and cook over medium heat for 5 minutes or until the butter is melted.

Unroll one pie crust, and place it on a baking sheet. Place in the oven. Bake for 5 minutes.

Remove the pie crust from the oven, and let cool.

Tear the baked pie crust into 2-inch square pieces.

In a large baking dish, combine the peach mixture and crumbled pie crust.

Spread some flour on the counter. On top of the flour, roll out the second pie crust. Cut it into 1-inch wide strips.

Place half the strips on top of the cobbler, facing the same direction with 1 inch between each strip. Place the remaining strips on top, perpendicular to the first half.

Place the baking dish in the oven. Bake for 25 minutes or until the crust is golden brown.

Enjoy!

Fried Apples

Prep time: 30 minutes
Cooking time: 35 minutes
Serves 10

Ingredients
3 granny smith apples
2 tablespoons lemon juice
1 stick salted butter
¾ cup sugar
1 teaspoon vanilla extract
½ teaspoon ground cinnamon
½ teaspoon nutmeg
2 cups whipped cream[10]

Directions
Peel and decore the apples. Slice apples into wedges. Put in a medium bowl . Pour lemon juice on top, and stir to prevent browning.
In a large skillet, melt the butter over medium heat. Add the apples, sugar, vanilla extract, cinnamon, and nutmeg. Stir well. Cook for 5 minutes or until apples are soft.
Serve with whipped cream.
Enjoy!

---

[10] See page 114 for recipe.

Double-Cookie Banana Pudding

Prep time: 30 minutes
Cooking time: 35 minutes
Serves 10

Ingredients

3–4 large bananas

2 7.25 ounce bags butter cookies

1 11ounce box vanilla wafer cookies

16 ounces whipped topping

4 cups milk

2 (5.1-ounce) banana cream pudding mix

Directions

Thinly slice bananas

In a large bowl, combine the pudding mix and milk. Whisk well for 3 minutes.

Fold the whipped topping into the pudding mix.

Line the bottom of a 9" X 12" casserole dish with the vanilla wafer cookies. Add a layer of bananas. Spread a layer of pudding approx.1 cup on top. Top with a layer of butter cookies. Repeat until cookies are gone, ending with the butter cookies.

Refrigerate for 2 hours.

Enjoy!

DIPS, SAUCES, AND GRAVIES

Bolognese Sauce

Prep time: 5 minutes
Cooking time: 10 minutes
Servings: 8 cups

Ingredients

1 pound ground beef
1 teaspoon ground parsley
2 teaspoons garlic powder
1 teaspoon black pepper

1 teaspoon Italian seasoning
1 teaspoon basil
1 28 oz jar thick and chunky marinara sauce
¼ cup medium salsa

Directions

To a large pot, add the ground beef. Season with the ground parsley, the garlic powder, black pepper, Italian seasoning, and basil. Cook over medium heat for approximately 5 minutes or until beef is brown, stirring occasionally.

Add the marinara sauce and salsa to the pot. Stir well and cook for an additional 5 minutes.

Refrigerate sauce overnight.

ENJOY!

Fruit Dip

Prep time: 10 minutes
Serves 4

This recipe creates three different dips. Eat with apple slices, strawberries, or other fruit.

Ingredients

¼ cup pecans

1 Heath bar

16 ounces whipped cream cheese

2 tablespoons caramel sauce, divided

1 tablespoon strawberry sauce

1 tablespoon chocolate sauce

Directions

Chop the pecans, and put them in a small bowl.

Chop the Heath bar, and put it in a separate bowl.

To a medium bowl, add the cream cheese and 1 tablespoon caramel sauce. Mix well.

Using an ice cream scooper, put one scoop of the cream cheese mixture in a small serving bowl. Add the remaining 1 tablespoon caramel sauce on top. Sprinkle ½ teaspoon pecans and ½ teaspoon Heath bar on top.

Put one scoop of the cream cheese mixture in a second small serving bowl. Top with the strawberry sauce, ½ teaspoon pecans, and ½ teaspoons Heath bar.

Put one scoop of the cream cheese mixture in a third small serving bowl. Top with the chocolate sauce, ½ teaspoon pecans, and ½ teaspoons Heath bar.

Enjoy!

Onion Gravy

Prep time: 5 minutes
Cooking time: 15 minutes
Makes 4 cups

This gravy can be used with so many things, from pouring it over meatloaf to meatballs.

Ingredients

1 large yellow onion
¾ stick butter
½ cup flour
32 ounces chicken broth or beef broth

3 teaspoons browning sauce
1 teaspoon kosher salt
1 teaspoon black pepper

Directions:

Julienne the onion.

In a medium saucepan, melt the butter. Add the onions, and sauté on medium heat for 5 minutes.

Add the flour to the saucepan with the onions, and cook for 5 minutes, whisking continuously.

Add the broth, browning sauce, salt, and black pepper to the saucepan, stirring constantly. Simmer over low heat for 5 minutes.

Remove from heat.

Enjoy!

Brown Gravy from Scratch

Prep time: 5 minutes
Cooking time: 10 minutes
Makes 2 cups

Ingredients

⅓ cup vegetable oil

⅓ cup all-purpose flour

½ teaspoon salt

½ teaspoon black pepper

½ teaspoon onion powder

1 (14.5-ounce) can chicken or beef broth

1 teaspoon browning sauce

Directions

In a medium sauté pan, heat oil over medium heat for 2 minutes.

Whisk the flour into the hot oil, stirring continuously until it browns.

Add the salt, black pepper, and onion powder to the pan.

Slowly stir in the broth and browning sauce. Whisk for 3 minutes to prevent lumps.

Simmer for five minutes.

Remove from heat, and enjoy.

Tomato Onion Gravy

Prep time: 5 minutes
Cooking time: 15 minutes
Makes 5 cups

This gravy has just enough spice and goes very well over the meat of your choice or rice.

Ingredients
1 large onion
¾ stick butter
½ cup flour
32 ounces chicken or beef broth
3 teaspoons browning sauce
1-10 ounce can diced tomatoes with green chilies
1 teaspoon kosher salt
1 teaspoon black pepper

Directions
Julienne the onion.
In a medium saucepan, melt the butter over medium heat. Add the onions, and sauté for 5 minutes.
Add the flour to the pan with the onions, and whisk for 5 minutes.
Add the broth to the pan. Stir constantly to make sure there are no lumps.
Add the browning sauce, stirring constantly.
Add the tomatoes. Season with the salt and black pepper. Cook for an additional 5 minutes.
Remove from the heat.
Enjoy!

Swedish Meatball Sauce

Prep time: 2 minutes
Cooking time: 5 minutes
Makes 2 cups

Ingredients

3 tablespoons butter
3 tablespoons flour
2 cups beef broth
1 teaspoon salt
1 teaspoon black pepper
¼ cup sour cream

Directions

Melt the butter in a medium skillet on low heat.

Add the flour to the melted butter. Stir until it's caramel colored.

Whisk in the broth, salt, and black pepper.

Stir in sour cream. Simmer on low heat for 3 minutes.

Homemade Sausage Gravy

Prep time: 5 minutes
Cooking time:15 minutes
Makes 2 cups

This homemade sausage gravy is not only quick and easy to prepare but tastes absolutely delicious on so many things, especially biscuits.

Ingredients

3 tablespoons vegetable oil

1-16 ounce tube hot breakfast sausage

1 teaspoon salt

1 teaspoon black pepper

1 teaspoon garlic powder

2 tablespoons flour

2 cups milk

Directions

Heat the oil in a medium skillet over high heat. Add the sausage, and cook until brown, stirring continuously. Season with the salt, black pepper, and garlic powder.

Add the flour to the skillet. Reduce heat to medium. Cook for 2 minutes, stirring continuously.

Add the milk. While stirring, simmer for 5 minutes or until thickened.

Enjoy!

Lemon Butter Cream Sauce

Cooking time:10 minutes

Makes 1 cup

This is a versatile sauce. It will bring a light, creamy taste to pasta, seafood, chicken, or vegetables.

Ingredients

½ stick butter

1 cup heavy whipping cream

¼ cup parmesan cheese

1 teaspoon salt

1 teaspoon lemon juice

Directions

In a medium saucepan, melt butter over medium heat. Whisk in the cream, and cook for 3 minutes.

Add the parmesan cheese and salt to the saucepan, whisking continuously.

Whisk in the lemon juice. Cook for 3–4 minutes or until thick.

Enjoy!

Cheesy Sausage Dip

Prep time: 10 minutes
Cooking time: 30 minutes
Serves 6

This dish goes great with chips or French bread.

Ingredients

16 ounces cream cheese

4 ounces extra sharp cheddar cheese

1 green onion

8 ounces Italian sausage

1 10 ounce can diced tomatoes with green chilies

1 teaspoon garlic powder

6 ounces Mexican cheese blend, divided

4 ounces mozzarella cheese, divided

Directions

Preheat oven to 375 degrees.

Dice the cream cheese and cheddar cheese. Slice the green onion.

In a medium saucepan, cook the suasage over medium heat until brown.

Add the tomatoes and garlic powder to the sausage. Combine well, and cook for 2 minutes.

In a medium baking dish, add the cream cheese, cheddar cheese, 4 ½ ounces Mexican cheese blend, and 3 ounces mozzarella cheese. Combine well.

Add the sausage mixture to the baking dish, and stir. Place the baking dish in the oven, and bake for 10 minutes.

Remove the dish from the oven, and stir well. Place back in the oven. Cook for an additional 15 minutes.

Remove the dish from the oven. Sprinkle the remaining 1 ½ ounces Mexican cheese blend and the remaining 1 ounce mozzarella cheese on top.

Set oven to broil. Place the dish back in the oven. Cook for 5 minutes.

Remove the dish from the oven. Top with the green onion slices.

Enjoy

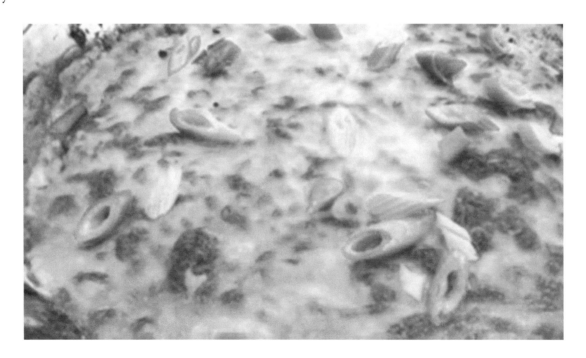

Grilled Shrimp and Avocado Salsa

Prep time: 5 minutes
Serves 4–6

Your family and guest will love this dip. The delicious grilled shrimp take it to the next level.

Ingredients

2 avocados

2 tomatoes

1 red onion

1 cucumber

1 jalapeño

2 tablespoons cilantro

1 lime

1 teaspoon salt

1 teaspoon black pepper

1 tablespoon creole seasoning

1 tablespoons vegetable oil

½ pound peeled and deveined shrimp

Directions

Remove the seed from the avocado. Peel and dice into small chunks. Dice the tomatoes, onion, and cucumber. Finely diced the jalapeño. Chop the cilantro.

In a large bowl, combine the tomatoes, onion, cucumber, jalapeño, and cilantro. Juice the lime on top. Season with the salt and black pepper. Mix well.

Season the shrimp with creole seasoning.

In a large skillet, heat the oil over high heat for 2 minutes. Add the shrimp, and cook for 30 seconds each on each side.

Remove the shrimp from the skillet, and let cool.

Add the shrimp and avocados to the bowl. Mix Well.

Enjoy!

Marinara Sauce

Prep time: 5 minutes
Cooking time: 15 minutes
Makes 3 cups

This is a slightly chunky sauce that will add an amazing flavor to any of your pasta dishes. The salsa is my secret ingredient.

Ingredients

2 (15-ounce) cans of tomato sauce
1 (6-ounce) can tomato paste
⅓ cup chunky medium salsa
1 teaspoon Italian seasoning
1 teaspoon garlic powder
1 teaspoon black pepper
1 teaspoon salt

Directions

In a saucepan, combine all ingredients, and mix well. Simmer over low heat for 15 minutes. Enjoy!

Pineapple Mango Salsa

Prep time: 5 minutes
Serves 4–6

This salsa isn't just for chips. It's great on fish and chicken as well.

Ingredients
1 fresh pineapple
1 fresh mango
1 red onion
1 jalapeño
2 tablespoons cilantro
1 lime

Directions
Peel and dice the pineapple and mango into small chunks. Finally dice the onion and jalapeño.[11] Chop the cilantro. In a large bowl, combine the pineapple, mango, onion, jalapeño, and cilantro. Juice the lime on top. Stir well. Cover the bowl, and place in the refrigerator. Let sit overnight.
Enjoy!

---

[11]   For a less spicy salsa, remove the seeds.

Rum Sauce

Prep time: 5 minutes
Cooking time: 5 minutes
Makes 2 cups

Ingredients

1 (14-ounce) can sweetened condensed milk
1 cup brown sugar, firmly packed
½ cup butter
⅛ teaspoon salt
¼ cup dark rum
2 tablespoons vanilla

Directions

In a medium saucepan, combine sweetened condensed milk, brown sugar, butter, and salt. Bring to a boil over medium heat, stirring constantly. Cook until sugar is dissolved.
Remove the saucepan from heat. Stir in the rum and vanilla.

APPETIZERS

Egg Rolls

Prep time: 25 minutes
Cooking time: 15 minutes
Serves 8

Ingredients

4 cups vegetable oil for frying wrapped eggrolls

4 tablespoons vegetable oil

4 cloves garlic, finely chopped

1 ½ tablespoons freshly grated ginger

1 cup carrots, finely chopped

2 scallions, thinly sliced

1 small red bell pepper, cut into 1-inch strips

1 pound ground turkey

1 teaspoon salt

1 teaspoon black pepper

1 teaspoon garlic powder

1 cup chicken broth

4 tablespoons soy sauce

2 tablespoons sugar

1 cup napa cabbage, shredded

2 tablespoons sesame oil

10 shrimp, cooked and minced

20 wonton wrappers

1 egg

1-8 ounce prepackaged bottle dipping sauce

1 cup chopped bok choy

Directions

To a wok, add 2 tablespoons vegetable oil over high heat. Add the garlic and ginger, and stir-fry for 30 seconds or until fragrant. Add the carrots, scallions, and red bell pepper. Cook for 2 minutes.

To a skillet, add the remaining 2 tablespoons vegetable oil and the ground turkey. Season with the salt, black pepper, and garlic powder. Stir to combine. Cook until brown.

In a medium bowl, combine the chicken broth, soy sauce, and sugar.

Add the Napa cabbage,bok choy and the broth mixture to the wok. Bring to a boil, and simmer for 5 minutes or until the vegetables are soft, stirring occasionally.

Add the sesame oil to the wok. Let cool for at least 15 minutes, and then strain.

Add the minced shrimp and turkey to the wok. Stir to combine.

In a small bowl, scramble the egg.

Lay one wonton wrapper flat with a corner close to you, making a diamond. Place 1 teaspoon of the filling in the center of the wrapper. Roll the closest corner over the filling. Brush the top corner with the egg. Fold in the sides, and continue rolling until it is closed. Press to seal, and set aside. Repeat until all wrappers are rolled.

In a seperate large skillet, heat the 4 cups oil over moderately high heat. Using tongs, fry the egg rolls until golden brown on all sides.

Serve with dipping sauce.

Enjoy!

Crab Wontons (Rangoons)

Prep time: 5 minutes
Cooking time: 5 minutes
Serves 6

Ingredients

4 cups vegetable oil
1 egg
1 teaspoon water
8 ounces cream cheese
¼ cup sliced green onions

1 tablespoon crab claw meat
1 teaspoon soy sauce
1-12 ounce package wonton wrappers
¼ teaspoon minced garlic

Directions

In a 4-quart Dutch oven heat the oil over high heat.

Soften the cream cheese in the microwave for 30 seconds.

In a bowl, combine the cream cheese, green onions, garlic, crabmeat, and soy sauce. Mix well.

In a small bowl, add the egg and water. Beat until combined to create an egg wash.

Lay out the wontons on the counter. Brush the egg wash on the outer edges.

Place one tablespoon of crab mixture in the center of each wonton. Fold the wontons over to make triangles, pressing the edges together.

Place four stuffed wontons into hot oil. Cook for 30 seconds. Flip and cook for an additional 30 seconds. Remove the wontons, and place on a plate lined with paper towels. Repeat until all wontons are fried.

Enjoy!

Crab-Stuffed Mushrooms (Red Lobster Copycat)

Prep time: 15 minutes
Cooking time: 20 minutes,
Serves 6

Ingredients

cooking oil spray

1 pound fresh button mushrooms

2 cups saltine crackers

1 cup shredded cheddar cheese, divided

8 ounces crab claw meat

¼ cup finely chopped celery

1 small red bell pepper, finely chopped

2 green onions, finely chopped

1 egg

½ teaspoon old bay seasoning

¼ teaspoon garlic powder

¼ teaspoon salt

¼ teaspoon black pepper

Directions

Preheat oven to 400 degrees. Spray a 9" X 12"casserole dish with cooking oil.

Wash the mushrooms, and remove the stems.[12]

In a large bowl, crush the crackers. Add ½ cup cheddar cheese, the crabmeat, celery, red bell pepper, green onions, and egg. Season with the old bay seasoning, garlic powder, salt, and black pepper. Mix well.

Stuff the mushroom caps with the crab mixture. Sprinkle a little cheese on top of each mushroom, and place in the casserole dish.

Place the casserole dish in the oven. Bake for 12 to 15 minutes or until cheese is lightly browned.

Remove the dish from the oven.

Enjoy!

---

[12] Save the stems to use in other recipes.

Cheesy Sausage-Stuffed Jalapeños

Prep time: 15 minutes
Cooking time: 25 minutes
Serves 4–6

Ingredients

cooking oil spray
4 fresh jalapeños
½ cup feta cheese

8 ounces cream cheese
1 16 ounce roll mild breakfast sausage

Directions

Preheat oven to 365 degrees. Spray a 9" X 12" baking sheet with cooking oil.

Slice the jalapeños lengthwise, and remove seeds. Line with the feta cheese.

Slice the cream cheese into small strips. Place one strip on top of each jalapeño.

Place 1 tablespoon sausage on top of each cream cheese jalepeno strip.

Place the peppers on the baking sheet. Put the baking sheet in the oven, and bake for 25 minutes.

Enjoy!

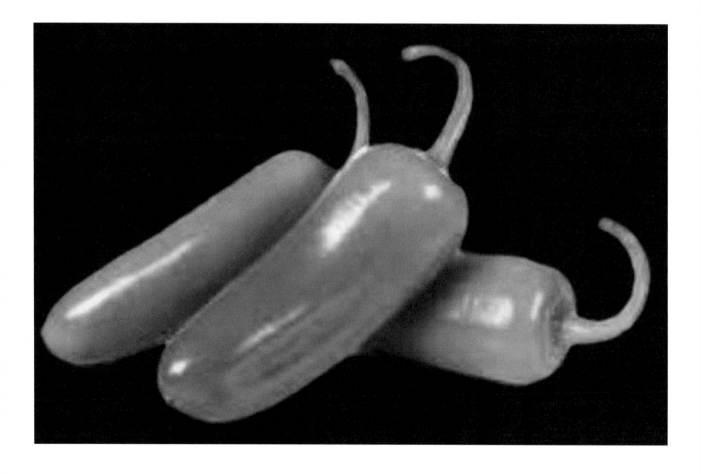

Fruit Tray

PrepTime: 45minutes

Serves: 25-30

These colorful fruit trays are show stoppers and will be the highlight of any party. The fresh and colorful fruits not only look great but taste great as well. You can make your fruit tray different every time by using different fruits or adding vegetables. Make your trays as small or as large as your party calls for.

Ingredients

8 ounces whipped topping

1-6 ounce package strawberry gelatin

2 cups cantaloupe

2 cups fresh pineapple

2 cups fresh strawberries

2 cups green grapes

2 cups red grapes

lettuce leaves to cover the tray

Directions

In a small decorative bowl, whisk together the whipped topping and strawberry gelatin. Set aside.

Wash all the fruit and lettuce thoroughly. Dice the cantaloupe and pineapple into 1-inch squares. Cut the stems off the strawberries.

Line a 21" X 15" tray with the lettuce leaves. Make sure the lettuce hangs over the edge of the tray by 1 inch.

Place the decorative bowl with the strawberry whipped topping in the middle of the tray.

Place a different fruit in each corner of the tray, making sure that it touches the bowl. Don't put two fruits of the same color are next to each other.

Fill any gaps along the sides of the tray with the remaining fruit. The fruit should be at least 2 inches high once you are finished.

Enjoy!

French Bread Avocado Toast

Prep time: 5 minutes
Cooking time: 3 minutes
Serves 4

Ingredients

1 loaf French bread

½ small red onion

2 tablespoons olive oil, divided

2 avocados

1 teaspoon lemon juice

½ teaspoon salt

½ teaspoon black pepper

½ teaspoon red pepper flakes

Directions

Set oven to broil.

Cut the bread into 2-inch pieces. Slice the onion into small slivers. Dice the avocados.

Brush half the oil on one side of the bread pieces. Place bread on a 9" X 12" baking sheet, and put in the oven. Broil for 3 minutes.

Add the diced avocados to a bowl. Combine with the remaining 1 tablespoon oil and the lemon juice. Season with the salt and black pepper. Fold together, keeping chunky.

Place a small scoop of the avocado mixture on each piece of toast. Sprinkle with red pepper flakes. Put one sliver of red onion on top.

Enjoy!

Glossary

Bake: To cook in an oven.

Beat: To mix ingredients together in a fast, circular movement with a spoon, fork, whisk, or mixer.

Blend: To gently mix ingredients together with a spoon or fork, until combined.

Boil: To heat a liquid hot enough for bubbles to rise and break the surface.

Broil: To cook under direct heat.

Brown: To cook over medium or high heat, until the surface of the food darkens or turns brown.

Chop: To cut into small pieces.

Dice: To cut into small cubes.

Drain: To remove all the liquid, either by using a colander or pressing a plate against the food while tilting the container.

Finely dice: To cut into very small pieces.

Grate: To scrape food against the holes of a grater, making thin pieces.

Grease: To lightly coat with oil, butter, margarine, or non-stick spray, so food does not stick when cooking or baking.

Knead: To press, fold, and stretch dough, until it is smooth and uniform. This is usually done by pressing with the heels of the hands.

Marinade: A liquid used for soaking food.

Marinate: To soak in a liquid to tenderize or add flavor.

Mash: To squash food with a fork, spoon, or masher.

Mince: To cut into very small pieces, smaller than chopped or diced.

Mix: To stir ingredients together with a spoon, fork, or electric mixer, until well combined.

Peel: To remove the skin.

Preheat: To heat oven ahead of time, so it is at the desired temperature when needed.

Rest: To let sit, covered.

Sauté: To quickly cook in a little oil, butter, or margarine.

Sear: To cook over high heat.

Season: To add seasonings to.

Shred: To scrape food against the smaller holes of a grater, making thin pieces

Simmer: To cook in liquid over low heat, so that bubbles just begin to break the surface.

Steam: To cook food over steam, without putting the food directly in the water.

Stir-fry: To quickly cook small pieces of food over high heat, stirring constantly, until the food is crispy and tender.

Translucent: semitransparent

Whisk: To beat or stir with a light, rapid movement.

Cooking Conversions

Dry Measurements

Cups	Tablespoons	Teaspoons	Ounces
1/16	1	3	1/2
1/8	2	6	1
1/4	4	12	2
1/3	5 1/3	16	3
1/2	8	24	4
2/3	10 2/3	32	5
3/4	12	36	6
1	16	48	8

Types of Onions

Green Onions are also known as scallions. They are onions taken from the ground before the bulb has formed. They are typically eaten raw and used as a garnish.

Red Onions are also known as purple onions. They have a purple-red skin and white flesh that is tinged with red. They are most often used in cooking, but their mild flavor makes them best eaten raw.

Shallots are small bulbs that resemble onions. They are used for pickling or as substitutes for onions. Shallots have a mild flavor. They are good for vinaigrettes and egg dishes.

Sweet Onions are also known as vidalia onions. They have thick layers and are good for making French onion soup and onion rings. They are mild, due to their low sulfur and high water content.

White Onions are sweet onions. They have a distinctly light and mild flavor. Much like red onions, they have a high water and sugar content. They are crunchy and have a short shelf life. White onions are mostly used in Mexican cooking.

Yellow Onions have a papery skin. Their high sulfur content gives them a strong, complex flavor. They caramelize well.

Notes

Notes

Notes

Notes

Printed in the United States
by Baker & Taylor Publisher Services